Blessing Prayers

Devotions for Growing in Faith

Father Peter John Cameron, O.P.

Edited by Andrew Matt

MAGNIFICAT®

Nihil Obstat: Monsignor Francis J. McAree, s.t.d.

Imprimatur: Bishop Dennis J. Sullivan

April 25, 2011

The Nihil Obstat and Imprimatur are official declarations that this book is free of doctrinal or moral error. No implication is contained therein that those who have granted the Nihil Obstat and Imprimatur agree with the content, opinions, or statements expressed.

Cover: *The Savior of the World,* Frans Pourbus the Elder (1545-1581), Saint Bavo Cathedral, Ghent, Belgium. © Bridgeman Giraudon.

Publisher: **Pierre-Marie Dumont**
Editor-in-Chief: **Peter John Cameron, o.p.**
Senior Editor: **Romanus Cessario, o.p.**
Managing Editor: **Catherine Kolpak**
Editorial Assistant: **Andrew Matt**
Administrative Assistants: **Jeanne Shanahan, Nora Macagnone**
Senior Managing Editor: **Frédérique Chatain**
Iconography: **Isabelle Mascaras**
Cover: **Solange Bosdevesy**
Layout: **Élise Borel, Facompo (Lisieux, France)**
Permissions: **Diaga Seck-Rauch**
Translator: **Janet Chevrier**

Table of Contents

Blessings for Spiritual Growth

Blessings and Prayers for Special Needs

A Word on Blessings

Father Peter John Cameron, O.P.

To utter a blessing is to acknowledge how much we have been blessed by God, even "with every spiritual blessing in the heavens" (Eph 1: 3). In the ancient Jewish tradition, every act and every pleasure called for a recognition of God's primary role as the Author of our needs and our wants. According to the Talmud, it is forbidden to enjoy anything of this world without saying a blessing. For this reason, the Jewish people composed blessings (*berakoth*) for every imaginable occasion: upon seeing lightning, upon seeing the ocean, upon seeing a rainbow, upon hearing good news, upon hearing bad news, during illness or recovery, when tired or dispirited, upon wearing a new garment, before a journey, when granted an escape from danger, etc.

No wonder, then, that the *Catechism of the Catholic Church* understands blessing as "a divine and life-giving action" that, when applied to human beings, "means adoration and surrender to [the] Creator in thanksgiving" (1078).

> Every blessing praises God and prays for his gifts... Every baptized person is called to be a "blessing," and to bless... *Blessing* expresses the basic movement of Christian prayer: it is an encounter between God and man. In blessing, God's gift and man's acceptance of it are united in dialogue with each other. The prayer of blessing is man's response to God's gifts: because God

blesses, the human heart can in return bless the One who is the source of every blessing. (CCC 1671, 1669, 2626)

Blessings lead us "to recognize the wholly loving creative initiative of God behind the precise action we are about to undertake and, by this very fact, to consecrate it to him" (Louis Bouyer). Because we trust in how much God loves us, we want him to be part of every dimension of our lives, even the most difficult and burdensome. In this spirit Christ commands us to "bless those who curse you" (Lk 6: 28). We invoke a blessing before whatever faces us in order to hand ourselves over totally to the Lord in love. And we do so with great confidence and certainty for, as Saint Ambrose instructs us, "the power of the blessing prevails over that of nature, because by the blessing nature itself is changed."

For all these reasons, when the Blessed Virgin Mary made her Visitation to her kinswoman Elizabeth, Elizabeth was moved to cry out, "Blessed are you among women" (Lk 1: 42). Her holy example verifies for us how much blessing is at the very heart of the *Magnificat* mystery.

Blessings for Liturgical Seasons

Blessing on
Our Advent Preparation

This blessing is based on the seven great "O" antiphons sung in the liturgy from December 17-24. The family might pray this blessing by gathering around the Advent wreath with different family members taking turns leading the various parts.

SUNDAY

O Wisdom, O Holy Word of God, you govern all creation with your strong yet tender care. Come and show your people the way to salvation.

The divine Wisdom that brought all creation into existence from nothing offers us a new beginning this Advent. The Word is spoken and comes to live among us in order to recreate us. "So whoever is in Christ is a new creation" (2 Cor 5: 17). "For neither does circumcision mean anything, nor does uncircumcision, but only a new creation" (Gal 6: 15). God has made Christ Jesus our Wisdom (see 1 Cor 1: 30) who keeps us in the Father's tender care.

> LORD JESUS, through the power of your strong yet tender care recreate me out of my nothingness this Advent. Bless the poor, the homeless, refugees, those who live without faith, the neglected, the marginalized, and those lost in sin. Show them the way to salvation.

MONDAY

O Sacred Lord of ancient Israel, who showed yourself to Moses in the burning bush, who gave him the Holy Law on Sinai mountain: come, stretch out your mighty hand to set us free.

Adonai, the God of the covenant, promises us this Advent the gift of the new covenant in Jesus Christ. The Father will show us his

Son through the Blessed Virgin Mary. Mary is prefigured in the burning bush because "she brought forth the power of the divine radiance without being consumed by it" (Rabanus Maurus). Christmas bestows us, not with a new law, but with the presence of the divine Lawgiver. He will "show us the Father" (Jn 14: 8) through his gift of self that empowers us with the freedom to know, love, and respond to God beyond our own natural capacities.

> LORD JESUS, free me this Advent from every inclination to self-absorption, willfulness, rebellion, disobedience, and dissent. Stretch out your mighty hand to set free the oppressed, the unjustly accused, captives, slaves, hostages, prisoners, and those enslaved by addictions.

TUESDAY

O Flower of Jesse's stem, you have been raised up as a sign for all peoples; kings stand silent in your presence; the nations bow down in worship before you. Come, let nothing keep you from coming to our aid.

Just as worldly kings stand in speechless awe before the divine Flower who is the fruit of Mary's womb, so will the world respond to those who witness to Jesus Christ. Father Jean-Pierre de Caussade, S.J., wrote, "Divine love, you can make fruitful the darkness in which you keep me. So my soul, like a tiny root, will stay hidden in you and your power will make it send forth fruit which will nourish and delight the souls of others."

> LORD JESUS, every day this Advent may I bow down in worship and prayer before you. Please bless the poor, the defenseless, the disabled, the unemployed, the sick, those experiencing financial difficulties, the unborn, the aged, and all those in need. Let nothing keep you from coming to their aid.

WEDNESDAY

O Key of David, O royal power of Israel, controlling at your will the gate of heaven: come, break down the prison walls of death for those who dwell in darkness and the shadow of death; and lead your captive people into freedom.

Through the Incarnation, Christ the Key unlocks the mysteries of heaven. The three mysteries of truth to inform our faith, of mercy to govern our hope, and of eternal life to direct our love come to us in Jesus through the Blessed Virgin Mary, the Gate of Heaven. What the Church declares loosed on earth will be loosed in heaven (Mt 16: 19) through the sacramental Keys that liberate every "captive to the law of sin" (Rom 7: 23).

> LORD JESUS, through confidence in hope help me to persevere when assailed by life's trials and turmoil. Bless all those who live in darkness and the shadow of death, and break down whatever imprisons them.

THURSDAY

O Radiant Dawn, splendor of eternal light, sun of justice: come, shine on those who dwell in darkness and the shadow of death.

"My soul looks for the Lord/ more than sentinels for daybreak" (Ps 130: 6). Our hearts are fixed hopefully on the dawn at Advent as they will be again at Easter. Even now we cry out for the resplendence revealed in Christ's Transfiguration. For the Messiah is "the sun of justice with its healing rays" (Mal 3: 20). He calls us "out of darkness into his wonderful light" (1 Pt 2: 9).

> LORD JESUS, illumine me with your luster that I may radiate your holiness this Advent and always. May the splendor of your eternal light shine on all those who suffer and on the dying.

FRIDAY

O King of all the nations, the only joy of every human heart; O keystone of the mighty arch of man: come and save the creature you fashioned from the dust.

The mark of a true king's greatness is his power to unify all things for the good of his subjects. Saint Thomas Aquinas tells us that people fall apart by their private interests and come together by their common ones. Joy is the fruit of such harmony. The key to Advent joy is surrendering all the disordered disharmony of our life to Christ the King by relying on Jesus the Keystone. And, since "no possession is joyous without a companion" (Saint Thomas), God gives us Mary, the New Eve, to be our Advent companion.

LORD JESUS, recreate me in your wisdom. Bless with comfort and joy the forgotten, the lonely, the broken-hearted, the abandoned, those who grieve and mourn, all those who are depressed, and those who have no one to pray for them.

SATURDAY

O Emmanuel, king and lawgiver, desire of the nations, savior of all people, come and set us free, Lord our God.

God wants to be with us. He places the desire for himself deep in the heart of every human being. God creates us in his image so that we might share his divine life. To experience the perfection of the divine likeness within us we must give ourselves fully to Christ as our Savior. Advent is the time to give up any delusions about possessing goodness outside of God. God's "plan of sheer goodness" in Emmanuel assures us not only that God is with us, but that God's goodness is what we are called to become.

LORD JESUS, purify my every desire so that I might share your life. Bless all civil leaders and legislators. Bless police officers, firefighters, and all those who risk their lives to protect us. Bless nations torn apart by hatred, oppression, and violence. Come and be with us.

A Day by Day Blessing for the
Advent Season

Most merciful Father, this Advent I desire to rededicate myself to the pursuit of holiness. May I live these days of grace united with the Blessed Virgin Mary in loving awareness of the presence of the One who changes us – Jesus your Son. In my vigilant expectation of Christ's coming, make me especially attentive to the wisdom of Sacred Scripture proclaimed in the liturgies of this holy season. May this blessed time of preparation be for me an occasion of conversion and spiritual rebirth. May each moment of my Advent bring me closer to you in faith, hope, and love through Emmanuel – Jesus Christ our Lord. Amen.

November 27

Father, let me live this Advent with a vigilant heart fixed on you. May I fulfill the great summons to "stay awake" by begging from moment to moment to do your holy will.

November 28

Father, may I make a gift of self to you this Advent. Instruct me in your ways so that I may always walk in your paths and go rejoicing to the house of the Lord.

November 29

Father, the great season of Advent looks forward to the day when the earth shall be filled with the knowledge of the Lord. Let me live always in that holy knowledge.

November 30

Father, in sending your Son you give us the Good Shepherd. Let me always remember that, though at times I walk in the dark valley, he is always at my side to give me courage.

December 1

Father, like clay in the hands of a potter, help me this Advent to place my life in your loving hands so to become refashioned according to your holy will.

December 2

Father, instruct me in your ways and strengthen my faith to trust always in your Word who comes to us with his healing power, despite our unworthiness.

December 3

Father, make me childlike in living my faith, and fill me with the Holy Spirit's gifts of wisdom, understanding, counsel, fortitude, piety, knowledge, and fear of the Lord.

December 4

Father, endow me with generous compassion for the poor and make me your instrument to wipe the tears away from all the faces of those who suffer in solitude.

December 5

Father, may I empty my life of all defiance, respond to the words your Son speaks to me, and trust your divine will with humble obedience and confidence.

December 6

Father, out of the gloom and darkness of my willfulness and arrogance, bless me with new hope to call upon the healing touch of Jesus your Son and our Savior.

December 7

Father, when the stranger of sin schemes to lead me astray, leaving me troubled and abandoned, show me Jesus the Way so that I may walk only in him.

DECEMBER 8

Father, as I prepare for the birth of your Son may I delight in the conception of his Blessed Mother and know in the miracle of Mary's immaculate flesh the promise of my own perfection.

DECEMBER 9

Father, envelop my life with your tenderness and comfort so that I can conduct myself with holiness and devotion, awaiting the coming of your Christ in security and peace.

DECEMBER 10

Father, strengthen me to fill in the valleys of my neglectfulness and to make low the mountains of my self-exaltation so as to prepare a straight highway for the Good Shepherd to find this lost sheep.

DECEMBER 11

Father, when I become oppressed by the labor and burdens of the world, help me to unite myself to your meek and humble Son who glories in making vigor abound for the weak.

DECEMBER 12

Father, help me remain in front of the mystery of the presence of your Son who comes to us through the Blessed Virgin Mary – the Mother of God whose love makes us your own.

DECEMBER 13

Father, free me from all my insolence and indignation, and empower me to confront my sins by hearkening to your life-giving commandments.

DECEMBER 14

Father, turn back my heart to all those you give me to love and care for, and help me to welcome all those you use to reveal your divine Son to me.

DECEMBER 15

Father, transform me so that I may rejoice always, pray without ceasing, give thanks in all circumstances, and refrain from every kind of evil, for you alone are the joy and the longing of my soul.

DECEMBER 16

Father, may I never doubt the authority of Jesus your Son but rather may I live abandoned to his lordship, seeing only what the Almighty sees, committed to integrity and truth.

DECEMBER 17

Father, liberate me from all the regrets, grudges, and sins of the past that continue to haunt my life; help me to recognize your unfailing providence in all things, and to worship you in heartfelt homage.

DECEMBER 18

Father, through the grace of the Gospel, salvation is born out of disappointment and heartache; be close to me so that I may face all of life's contradictions with conviction and simplicity.

DECEMBER 19

Father, my life is nothing but barrenness without the fruit of Mary's womb, Jesus; assist me these Decembers before the Nativity so that I might surrender myself to grace-filled, saving silence.

DECEMBER 20

Father, may the fearlessness and faith of the Blessed Virgin fill me so that I can empty my life of all doubt, sarcasm, pettiness, cynicism, and complaining.

DECEMBER 21

Father, like blessed Elizabeth, so often I feel insecure and inadequate, unworthy of the gift of the visit of the Mother of your

Son; embolden me to welcome Mary without reserve because she comes to assure me that I am your beloved one.

DECEMBER 22

Father, give me rest from all my enemies; rescue me from shameful secrets that keep me miserable, and make my soul resound with the greatness of the Lord that Mary proclaims.

DECEMBER 23

Father, your Son comes to save us from our sins; turn my heart back to you so that I may recognize at every moment my need to be refined and redeemed.

DECEMBER 24

Father, your Son Jesus Christ reveals me to myself; as I dwell in the darkness of this Christmas Eve, guide me out of all slavery, vice, and sin into the way of the Prince of Peace.

DECEMBER 25

Father, with all my heart, soul, mind, and strength help me to love the humanity of your Son so that I might share in his divinity and become a child truly fit for heaven.

Our Father...

The Blessing of
Salvation History

The Incarnation of Jesus Christ is the fulfillment of a great promise that God made to his people. Salvation history is filled with saintly people who played an instrumental role in realizing the supreme promise of God (see Mt 1: 1-17; Lk 3: 23-38). A suggestion for this Advent is to begin your Nativity scene early and to expand it. Designate one place as "Eden" and from it trace a path to the manger in Bethlehem. Insert along the way figures of some of the holy heroes of salvation history – such as the ones suggested below – who prepare us for the coming of Christ, beginning with Adam and Eve. Each day recite the blessing prayer that celebrates the historical way that divine providence makes straight the path for the birth of the Son of God.

NOVEMBER 27

Loving Father, as a result of the sin of Adam and Eve we cry out for the coming of your Son; perfect my obedience this Advent.

NOVEMBER 28

Loving Father, Noah built an ark to withstand the destructive waters of the flood; deepen my love of the Church this Advent.

NOVEMBER 29

Loving Father, you promised a covenant to Abraham; strengthen my trust in your providence this Advent.

NOVEMBER 30

Loving Father, the priest Melchizedek foreshadowed Jesus the great High Priest; strengthen and purify your priests this Advent.

December 1

Loving Father, through the design of Rebekah, Isaac her husband blessed their younger son; bless me with your love this Advent.

December 2

Loving Father, Jacob wrestled with an angel; bless me with your fatherly presence and protection this Advent.

December 3

Loving Father, despite murderous betrayal, Joseph sought reconciliation with his brothers; reconcile my family this Advent.

December 4

Loving Father, Moses freed his people from the slavery of Egypt; free me from whatever enslaves me this Advent.

December 5

Loving Father, tradition says that, at the Exodus from Egypt, Nahshon walked head deep into the Red Sea until the waters parted. Bless my Advent with new initiatives of grace.

December 6

Loving Father, Ruth said to Naomi, "Wherever you go I will go"; deepen my friendships this Advent.

December 7

Loving Father, when the young Samuel heard God calling his name in his sleep, Samuel arose longing to do God's willl. Let me live by your will this Advent.

December 8

Loving Father, the prostitute Rahab gave refuge to your servants in peril; may the Virgin Mary's immaculate love be a refuge for me this Advent.

DECEMBER 9

Loving Father, you made Saul the first king of Israel; may I live committed to your kingship this Advent.

DECEMBER 10

Loving Father, Jesse was the father of David; may the fruitfulness of the Jesse Tree revitalize my spiritual life this Advent.

DECEMBER 11

Loving Father, David slew the giant Goliath; unite me to those who call out for the power of the Son of David this Advent.

DECEMBER 12

Loving Father, the wise King Solomon built for you a temple; may I reverence my body as a temple of the Holy Spirit this Advent.

DECEMBER 13

Loving Father, your prophet Isaiah proclaimed, "'Give comfort to my people,' says your God"; fill me with your comfort this Advent.

DECEMBER 14

Loving Father, the prophet Jonah emerged alive after three days in the belly of a fish; revive my life in every way this Advent.

DECEMBER 15

Loving Father, through your prophet Hosea you promised, "I will espouse you to me for ever"; fill me with sincere sorrow for my sins this Advent.

DECEMBER 16

Loving Father, you carried your mighty prophet Elijah up to heaven in a fiery chariot; may I be caught up in the fire of your love this Advent.

DECEMBER 17

Loving Father, your prophet Jeremiah declared, "Before I formed you in the womb I knew you"; may the culture of life transform the world this Advent.

DECEMBER 18

Loving Father, when Shadrach, Meshach, and Abednego were cast into the fiery furnace, they were consoled by the mysterious presence of one who looked like a son of God. May I spend my Advent adoring your Son.

DECEMBER 19

Loving Father, to a people in exile your prophet Ezekiel preached hope; restore and transform me this Advent.

DECEMBER 20

Loving Father, the courage of Queen Esther rescued your people from destruction; may Mary's maternal mediation sanctify me this Advent.

DECEMBER 21

Loving Father, Saints Joachim and Anne were the parents of the Blessed Virgin Mary; relieve me from depression and despondency this Advent.

DECEMBER 22

Loving Father, Saint Joseph believed the dream of an angel; may I prayerfully welcome Mary as your miraculous gift to me this Advent.

DECEMBER 23

Loving Father, John the Baptist leapt in his mother's womb at the presence of your Son; make me a missionary of the Gospel this Advent.

DECEMBER 24

Loving Father, you gave us your beloved Son through the Blessed Virgin Mary; bless me with the virtues of the Mother of God this Advent.

DECEMBER 25

Loving Father, your Son Jesus is the Word made flesh; may my Advent become an unceasing encounter with the Event of Christ's unending presence.

Blessing before a
Christmas Stable

"No one, whether shepherd or wise man, can approach God here below except by kneeling before the manger at Bethlehem and adoring him hidden in the weakness of a new-born child."

Catechism of the Catholic Church, 563

Lord Jesus, as I kneel before your manger in adoration, let my first Christmas word be: *thank you.* Thank you, Gift of the Father, for coming to save me from my sins.

Without you I do not know even how to be human. The characteristics of your human body express the divine person of God's Son. And in that wondrous expression, Lord, you reveal me to myself. Thank you for that saving revelation in your sacred humanity. As the Christmas liturgy proclaims, "in Christ man restores to man the gift of everlasting life." Thank you for coming as one like myself to save me from myself.

You come as a baby because babies are irresistible and adorable. You come as a baby because you want our first impression of God incarnate to be that of one who does not judge. How I long to be united with you in every way. May I never be attracted to the allurements and charms of the world. May I love you always, at every moment, with all my heart, soul, mind, and strength. May the tenderness, the dependency, and the mercy that you reveal in your infancy become the hallmarks of my life.

Newborn Savior, the very silence of your Incarnation proclaims that the answer to the misery, the strife, and the meaninglessness we often experience in life cannot be found within us. You alone are the Answer. As I kneel before you, eternal King, I surrender to you all my selfishness, self-absorption, self-indulgence, self-righteousness, self-assertion, and self-exaltation. Even as I adore you on this night of your birth, rid me of the nagging desire to be adored.

Word become flesh, you make your dwelling among us. Yet you do not live your life for yourself, but for us. And you enable us to live in you all that you yourself lived. Help me to embrace this truth with all my mind and heart. Come and live your life in me. Empty me of my willfulness, my petulance, my hardness, my cynicism, my contemptuousness. Fill me with your truth, your strength, your fortitude, your purity, your gentleness, your generosity, your wisdom, your heart, and your grace.

O Emmanuel, may the assurance of your unfailing Presence be for me the source of unending peace. May I never fear my weakness, my inadequacy, or my imperfection. Rather, as I gaze with faith, hope, and love upon your incarnate littleness, may I love my own littleness, for God is with us. Endow my life with a holy wonder that leads me ever more deeply into the Mystery of Redemption and the meaning of my vocation and destiny.

Longed-for Messiah, your servant Saint Leo the Great well wrote that in the very act of reverencing the birth of our Savior, we are also celebrating our own new birth. From this night on may my life be a dedicated life of faith marked by holy reliance, receptivity, and resoluteness. May I make of my life a total gift of self. May my humble worship of your Nativity manifest how much I seek the Father's kingship and his way of holiness. The beauty of your holy face bears the promise that your Father will provide for us in all things. This Christmas I renew my trust in God's goodness, compassion, and providence. I long for the day when you will teach us to pray "Our Father."

May your Presence, Prince of Peace, bless the world with peace, the poor with care and prosperity, the despairing with hope and confidence, the grieving with comfort and gladness, the oppressed with freedom and deliverance, the suffering with solace and relief. Loving Jesus, you are the only real joy of every human heart. I place my trust in you.

O divine Fruit of Mary's womb, may I love you in union with the holy Mother of God. May my life be filled with the obedience of Saint Joseph and the missionary fervor of the shepherds so that the witness of my life may shine like the star that leads the Magi to your manger. I ask all this with great confidence in your holy name. Amen.

Blessing on
Christmas Presents

"Much of the richness and complexity of the mystery of the Lord's manifestation is reflected in displays of popular piety, which is especially sensitive to the childhood of Christ which reveals his love for us. Popular piety intuitively grasps the importance of the 'spirituality of gift', which is proper to Christmas: 'a child is born for us, a son is given to us' (see Is 9: 5), a gift expressing the infinite love of God, who 'so loved the world that he gave his only Son' (Jn 3: 16)."

Directory on Popular Piety and the Liturgy, 108

This blessing might be recited before or after going to Christmas Mass, before Christmas dinner, as part of the family's prayer at night on Christmas, or at any other time during Christmas Day or Christmastide.

Word of God   Psalm 103: 1-5

BLESS THE LORD, my soul;/ all my being, bless his holy name!/ Bless the LORD, my soul;/ do not forget all the gifts of God,/ Who pardons all your sins,/ heals all your ills,/ Delivers your life from the pit,/ surrounds you with love and compassion,/ Fills your days with good things;/ your youth is renewed like the eagle's.

LITANY OF CHRISTMAS THANKS

℟ Baby Jesus, we thank you.

◄ For the Blessed Virgin Mary your Mother who said "Yes" to the angel: ℟

◄ For John the Baptist who leapt in the womb of Elizabeth his mother when you visited him in Mary: ℟

‹ For Joseph your foster father who trusted the angel instead of heeding his own doubts: ℟

‹ For the donkey that carried your expectant Mother to Bethlehem: ℟

‹ For the neighbor who led your holy family to the stable: ℟

‹ For the manger in which you were placed as if in the first tabernacle: ℟

‹ For the animals who were there in the first moments that you were adored: ℟

‹ For the angels and their song that led shepherds to your stable: ℟

‹ For the shepherds who worshiped you and then proclaimed the Good News like priests: ℟

‹ For Simeon who all his life had been waiting for you in the temple, longing to hold you: ℟

‹ For Anna the prophetess who proclaimed you to all those looking for deliverance and peace: ℟

‹ For the star that led the Magi to your manger and your Mother: ℟

Closing Prayer

Loving Father, all of these Christmas gifts symbolize how much you love us with the supreme Gift of your Son, Jesus Christ, born for us this Christmas Day. We give these gifts to one another to express how grateful we are for your unfathomable generosity and to show how eager we are to share that goodness with one another. Bless these tokens of love and caring. Never let us get attached to material things, but rather let the joy flowing from these presents strengthen our bonds of love, deepen our relationships, and move us to be more thankful, selfless, and giving all the days of our life. Thank you for the birth of Jesus, our brother and our Savior.

Blessing to Pray on
New Year's Day

"But when the fullness of time had come,
God sent his Son, born of a woman."
(Gal 4: 4)

Word of God   **Hebrews 1: 10-12**

AT THE BEGINNING, O Lord, you established the earth,/ and the heavens are the works of your hands./ They will perish, but you remain;/ and they will all grow old like a garment./ You will roll them up like a cloak,/ and like a garment they will be changed./ But you are the same, and your years will have no end.

LITANY OF THE NEW YEAR

℞ **Father, give us this day our daily bread.**

‹ For the grace to live in the present moment: ℞

‹ For the ability to recognize divine providence in what appears to be coincidence: ℞

‹ On all new resolutions to live by faith in the pursuit of happiness: ℞

‹ For the strength to honor all my promises and commitments: ℞

‹ For a rectified use of my time: ℞

‹ For wisdom to set proper priorities and schedules: ℞

‹ On all new projects: ℞

‹ For the virtue to be determined and deliberate in all my dealings: ℞

‹ For thankfulness when offered a second chance: ℞

‹ For the will not to procrastinate: ℟

‹ For the insight to make new plans well and to follow them through faithfully: ℟

‹ For constancy in consecrating time to God each day: ℟

‹ For the discipline not to waste time or to dawdle or trifle: ℟

‹ For the courage to have hope in facing the future: ℟

‹ For the ability to be on time: ℟

‹ For freedom from rushing and franticness: ℟

‹ For the grace to savor the gift of time: ℟

‹ For the right respect of deadlines and due dates: ℟

‹ For devotion only to what really matters: ℟

‹ That God will be the Lord of my mornings: ℟

‹ That God will be the Lord of my afternoons: ℟

‹ That God will be the Lord of my evenings and nights: ℟

‹ For blessings on all new beginnings: ℟

Closing Prayer

MOST MERCIFUL FATHER, with the Lord one day is like a thousand years and a thousand years like one day. Throughout every moment of this New Year, keep me united with the Lord Jesus Christ so that I might live fully alive in the power of the Eternal Day of your Son's Resurrection. I ask this through Christ our Lord.

Blessing for the
Keeping of Lent

"Lent is a privileged time of interior pilgrimage towards him who is the fount of mercy… Even in the 'valley of darkness'… while the tempter prompts us to despair… God is there to guard us and sustain us. In the desolation of misery, loneliness, violence, and hunger that indiscriminately afflict children, adults, and the elderly, God does not allow darkness to prevail. The gaze of Jesus embraces individuals and multitudes, and he brings them all before the Father, offering himself as a sacrifice of expiation. In turning to the Divine Master, in being converted to him,… we will discover a 'gaze' that searches us profoundly and gives new life to… each one of us. It restores trust to those who do not succumb to skepticism."

Pope Benedict XVI

During Lent we want to "give up" anything that smacks of the common mentality – all our negativity and fatalism, anything that stalls our spiritual growth, that discourages or misleads us, or that makes us lose heart when it comes to our relationship with God. So many misconceptions and erroneous notions lead us astray and deprive us of hope. In particular, we need to have a right understanding of the role that our limitations, our fragility, and even our failings play in our sanctification according to divine providence. This Lent we offer up to the Lord all our pessimism, self-doubt, and self-defeat. The resurrected Christ rises out of our nothingness.

WORD OF GOD

SUNDAY

We were utterly weighed down beyond our strength, so that we despaired even of life. Indeed, we had accepted within ourselves the sentence of death, that we might trust not in ourselves but in God who raises the dead. He rescued us from such great danger of death, and he will continue to rescue us. (2 Cor 1: 8-10a)

MONDAY

We are afflicted in every way, but not constrained; perplexed, but not driven to despair; persecuted, but not abandoned; struck down, but not destroyed; always carrying about in the body the dying of Jesus, so that the life of Jesus may also be manifested in our body. (2 Cor 4: 8-10)

TUESDAY

Therefore, we are not discouraged; rather, although our outer self is wasting away, our inner self is being renewed day by day. For this momentary light affliction is producing for us an eternal weight of glory beyond all comparison, as we look not to what is seen but to what is unseen. (2 Cor 4: 16-18a)

WEDNESDAY

I rejoice now, not because you were saddened, but because you were saddened into repentance; for you were saddened in a godly way, so that you did not suffer loss in anything because of us. For godly sorrow produces a salutary repentance without regret. (2 Cor 7: 9-10a)

THURSDAY

That I might not become too elated, a thorn in the flesh was given to me, an angel of Satan, to beat me, to keep me from being too elated. Three times I begged the Lord about this, that it might leave me, but he said to me, "My grace is sufficient for you, for power is made perfect in weakness." I will rather boast most gladly of my weaknesses, in order that the power of Christ may dwell with me. (2 Cor 12: 7-9)

FRIDAY

I am content with weaknesses, insults, hardships, persecutions, and constraints, for the sake of Christ; for when I am weak, then I am strong. (2 Cor 12: 10)

SATURDAY

For indeed [Christ] was crucified out of weakness, but he lives by the power of God. So also we are weak in him, but toward you we shall live with him by the power of God.

Examine yourselves to see whether you are living in faith. (2 Cor 13: 4-5a)

LITANY OF SPIRITUAL CONFIDENCE

℟ Lord, keep me close to you.

‹ Lord, I can do all that you ask of me because it is you who strengthen me. ℟

‹ Lord, whenever I fall you delight in my confidence to trust you all the more. ℟

‹ Lord, let me look to you and not to myself to find what is needed to please you. ℟

‹ Lord, when I am overcome by fear it is because my peace depends on some thing instead of on your will. ℟

‹ Lord, free me from my hidden attachments to self-righteousness. ℟

‹ Lord, let me always remember that it is you who move me to ask for your love. ℟

‹ Lord, help me to see that the meaning of my faults is to learn to depend on you more and more. ℟

‹ Lord, give me the strength to cry out for your love when all that I see is nothingness in myself. ℟

‹ Lord, save me from the impulse to look for my peace and security in my own strength. ℟

‹ Lord, the more you let me see what I am left to myself, the more you give me the grace to cling to you. ℟

‹ Lord, to be happy, I need nothing but what you provide for me at every moment. ℟

‹ Lord, the more I live in the love you give me in this moment, the more perfectly I am able to suffer whatever comes my way. ℟

‹ Lord, when I come to you at those times when I am overwhelmed by my own misery I glorify you the most. ℟

‹ Lord, it is in being receptive to you in the knowledge of my own weakness that I derive all my strength. ℟

‹ Lord, let me always remember that you want me to let you make me perfect by your love. ℟

‹ Lord, the measure of my union with you is my faith in the power of your love to purify me and make me worthy of you. ℟

A Day-by-Day Blessing for
Lent

We sanctify each day of the holy season of Lent by listening attentively to the words of Jesus and obediently following his voice. After each daily invocation, recite the prayer at the end of the blessing, followed by the Our Father.

DAY 1: "Pray to your Father who is in secret."

Lord, let me live this Lent as one great act of adoration. My prayer is a begging to know the meaning of my life so that I may live it totally for you.

DAY 2: "If any man would come after me, let him … take up his cross."

Lord, the presence of your cross in my life is a gift of the Father that separates me from whatever separates me from God. Let me embrace it with all my strength.

DAY 3: "When the bridegroom is taken away from them, then they will fast."

Lord, may my fasting this Lent be a symbol of my longing to be filled with your presence. In the food of the Eucharist I find my salvation.

DAY 4: "Follow me."

Lord, may the loving gaze of your face move me to leave behind everything in my life that keeps me from living for you. Let me follow you in faith.

DAY 5: "Come, O blessed of my Father."

Lord, make my whole life a response to your invitation of love; may each moment today draw me closer into your embrace.

DAY 6: "Forgive men their trespasses."

Lord, presumption – the second worst sin – blights my life when I refuse to forgive; make me generous in extending your mercy to those who deserve it least.

DAY 7: "No sign shall be given."

Lord Jesus, more than any sign, your presence is what corresponds to the deepest longings of my heart; help me to remain attentive to your presence always.

DAY 8: "Seek, and you will find."

Lord, human life is searching and aspiration; perfect my efforts at prayer so that the entreaty of my life will always please you.

DAY 9: "Go; first be reconciled."

Lord, give me the grace to take the initiative to repair any relationships in my life that are broken or neglected.

DAY 10: "Be perfect, as your heavenly Father is perfect."

Lord, bless me to live free of doubt, deeply believing in the possibility of perfection – my promised destiny.

DAY 11: "The measure you give will be the measure you get back."

Lord, purge my life of every false measure by which I would attempt to impose something less than Mystery as the standard for happiness.

DAY 12: "Whoever humbles himself will be exalted."

Lord, empower me to live the truth that holiness means depending on you in simplicity and surrender.

DAY 13: "The Son of Man [… came] to give his life as a ransom."

Lord, enable me to make a sincere gift of myself in concrete ways to others today out of love for you.

DAY 14: "Neither will they be convinced if some one should rise from the dead."

Lord, the human heart is enlightened by tenderness and converted by looking at your cross; make me tender and repentant today.

DAY 15: "The kingdom of God will be [...] given to a nation producing the fruits of it."

Lord, the fruit of the kingdom is the obedience that began when your Mother said Yes to the Father; fill me with that same obedience that I too may be the fruit of Mary's womb.

DAY 16: "All that is mine is yours."

Lord Jesus, strip me of all my pettiness so that nothing will lessen my longing to return to the Father, my Everything.

DAY 17: "No prophet is acceptable in his own country."

Lord, give me the courage to be a true prophet – one who announces the significance of the world and the value of life.

DAY 18: "Forgive your brother from your heart."

Lord, fill me with holy forgetting of offenses committed against me, and make forgiveness the controlling impetus of my life.

DAY 19: "Whoever does [these commandments] and teaches them shall be called great in the kingdom of heaven."

Lord, from all defiance, self-dependence, and self-assertion release me that I may love the wisdom of your law.

DAY 20: "Every kingdom divided against itself is laid waste."

Lord, I lay before you today all the rebellion and indignation that otherwise divide me in my very self.

DAY 21: "Did you not know that I must be in my Father's house?"

Lord, may the paternity of Saint Joseph enable me to penetrate to the heart of your will which I long to fulfill with all the affection that Joseph bore to his spouse Mary.

DAY 22: The [tax collector] went down to his house justified.

Lord, rid my life of all the pride and self-righteousness that make me scornful of your humanizing gift of mercy.

DAY 23: "Your son will live."

Lord, in the face of despair and the impossible make me steadfast in trusting your commands.

DAY 24: "Do you want to be healed?"

Lord, cure me of all fatalism, negativity, cynicism, and defeatism.

DAY 25: "He who hears my word […] has eternal life."

Lord, help me to listen better today, that in my encounter with your Word I might experience here and now heaven.

DAY 26: "Hail, full of grace!"

Lord, may the courage with which the Blessed Virgin Mary received these words fill me with confidence to stay close to your cross from which you command, "Behold your Mother."

DAY 27: "He who sent me is true."

Lord, generate me with the love of your Father who sends you to me in order to save me from the falsehood and lies of myself.

DAY 28: Others [who heard these words of Jesus] said, "This is the Christ."

Lord, the power of your words transforms a crowd into a communion; deepen my bonds to those who believe in your words.

DAY 29: "If you had known me, you would have known my Father also."

Lord Jesus, the only genuine way to know you is as a child, for then I am certain that I know and love the Father; help me to live spiritual childhood perfectly.

DAY 30: "You will die in your sins."

Lord, the world is expert at treating sin like a fiction; may I know sin's true horror, and in that knowledge fly to your mercy.

DAY 31: "The truth will make you free."

Lord Jesus, freedom is the capacity for the infinite; help me to adhere only to the truth that brings about unfailing friendship with you.

DAY 32: "If any one keeps my word, he will never taste death."

Lord, your Word creates me and recreates me. Let me hear your voice and be ever obedient to you.

DAY 33: "I am in the Father and the Father in me."

Lord, every one of your works reveals the Father to the world. May I be united with the Father's will in all my daily works.

DAY 34: So from that day on they took counsel how to put [Jesus] to death.

Lord, the world cannot remain indifferent before you, for we were made for the love that you alone make incarnate. Free me from every trace of defiance.

DAY 35: "Mary […] anointed the feet of Jesus."

Lord, as the time of your crucifixion draws near, let me be united with you through a renewal of faith and a true dying to self.

DAY 36: "I will lay down my life for you."

Lord, my desire to sacrifice myself for you can be so easily undone by my cowardice. Let the union I have lived with you this Lent save me from what is lacking in my sinful self.

DAY 37: "One of you will betray me."

Lord, the example of Judas Iscariot reveals to the world that none of us is exempt from the temptation of betraying you. I profess my love to you anew this day. Keep my safe from my own treachery.

DAY 38: Jesus loved his own who were in the world […] to the end.

Lord, you express your ineffable love through the gesture of washing our feet, instituting the Holy Eucharist, and establishing the priesthood. Let me live this love at every moment.

DAY 39: "Behold, your mother!"

Lord, even as you are dying on the cross you bless us with new ways of loving us. The faith of the Blessed Virgin Mary gives us eyes to see beyond the horror of Calvary. Let me live this faith at every moment.

DAY 40: At early dawn, they went to the tomb.

Lord, the women who kept vigil at the tomb knew that the only thing that makes sense in life is to stay close to you. Let me live this hope at every moment.

CLOSING PRAYER

MOST MERCIFUL FATHER, may every day of the season of Lent be for me an act of sacrifice. Allow me to penetrate everything that I love with the memory of Jesus your Son, so that everything that I love will become truer and pure through the encounter with the crucified Christ, who is our Lord, now and for ever.

Lenten Blessing to
Help Carry Our Cross

"Worship him who was hung on the cross because of you, even if you are hanging there yourself."

Saint Gregory Nazianzen

The cross is a great privilege for it blesses us with the assurance of what really matters in life – what is REAL. *The cross gives us the opportunity to encounter reality and to enter into reality like Christ and with Christ. Without the constant, daily experience of the cross, we would lose touch with this saving reality and become lax in our understanding and efforts. We ask the Lord to bless all our experiences of the cross this day and throughout the holy season of Lent.*

WORD OF GOD

SUNDAY

The message of the cross is foolishness to those who are perishing, but to us who are being saved it is the power of God. (1 Cor 1: 18)

MONDAY

But may I never boast except in the cross of our Lord Jesus Christ, through which the world has been crucified to me, and I to the world. (Gal 6: 14)

TUESDAY

For he is our peace, he who made both one and broke down the dividing wall of enmity, through his flesh, abolishing the law with its commandments and legal claims, that he might create in himself one new person in place of the two, thus establishing peace, and might reconcile both with God, in one body, through the cross, putting that enmity to death by it. (Eph 2: 14-16)

WEDNESDAY

We are afflicted in every way, but not constrained; perplexed, but not driven to despair; persecuted, but not abandoned; struck down, but not destroyed; always carrying about in the body the dying of Jesus, so that the life of Jesus may also be manifested in our body. For we who live are constantly being given up to death for the sake of Jesus, so that the life of Jesus may be manifested in our mortal flesh. (2 Cor 4: 8-11)

THURSDAY

Therefore, since we are surrounded by so great a cloud of witnesses, let us rid ourselves of every burden and sin that clings to us and persevere in running the race that lies before us while keeping our eyes fixed on Jesus, the leader and perfecter of faith. For the sake of the joy that lay before him he endured the cross, despising its shame, and has taken his seat at the right of the throne of God. (Heb 12: 1-2)

FRIDAY

For his sake I have accepted the loss of all things and I consider them so much rubbish, that I may gain Christ and be found in him, not having any righteousness of my own based on the law but that which comes through faith in Christ, the righteousness from God, depending on faith to know him and the power of his resurrection and [the] sharing of his sufferings by being conformed to his death. (Phil 3: 8-10)

SATURDAY

He himself bore our sins in his body upon the cross, so that, free from sin, we might live for righteousness. By his wounds you have been healed. (1 Pt 2: 24)

LITANY OF THE GRACES OF THE CROSS

℟ **Because by your holy cross you have redeemed the world.**

‣ We adore you, O Christ, when we do not get our own way: ℟

‣ We adore you, O Christ, in the midst of day to day aggravations, frustrations, and annoyances: ℟

‣ We adore you, O Christ, when we live deprived of recognition or gratitude: ℟

‣ We adore you, O Christ, when dealing with others who exalt themselves and demean us: ℟

‣ We adore you, O Christ, when injustice gets us down: ℟

‣ We adore you, O Christ, in the face of worry, anxiety, and fear: ℟

‣ We adore you, O Christ, when we forgive others and show them mercy, especially when it hurts: ℟

‣ We adore you, O Christ, in the face of others' thoughtlessness: ℟

‣ We adore you, O Christ, in confronting our daily inner rebellion: ℟

‣ We adore you, O Christ, in refusing to give in to vanity and self-importance: ℟

‣ We adore you, O Christ, in always thinking about others first and putting them first: ℟

‣ We adore you, O Christ, when others take us for granted: ℟

‣ We adore you, O Christ, when suffering the agony of depression: ℟

‣ We adore you, O Christ, in our inability to make sense out of life or to have things follow our plans, especially when we're trying so hard to be good: ℟

‹ We adore you, O Christ, in rejecting self-assertion and self-satisfaction: ℟

‹ We adore you, O Christ, in the midst of the oppressiveness of life – its futility, drudgery, pointlessness, and tedium: ℟

‹ We adore you, O Christ, in letting go of the order and control we crave: ℟

‹ We adore you, O Christ, when accosted by the unfairness of seeing the wicked succeed: ℟

‹ We adore you, O Christ, despite the world's contradiction, humiliation, and derision: ℟

‹ We adore you, O Christ, by refusing to live according to our feelings: ℟

‹ We adore you, O Christ, when we are under-appreciated: ℟

‹ We adore you, O Christ, when our egoism and willfulness flare up: ℟

‹ We adore you, O Christ, when we are persecuted for your sake: ℟

‹ We adore you, O Christ, even when confronted by crisis and catastrophe: ℟

‹ We adore you, O Christ, as we live by love and no lesser motive: ℟

‹ We adore you, O Christ, in finding peace in the total surrender of self: ℟

‹ We adore you, O Christ, in accepting that God works in the ways we least expect: ℟

‹ We adore you, O Christ, as we search for self-worth only in God's love for us and nothing else: ℟

Blessing for the
Graces of the Easter Tomb

This blessing might be prayed in front of the baptismal font, the paschal candle, or before a replica of the holy sepulcher erected in your church for Easter.

WORD OF GOD

SUNDAY

"The hour is coming in which all who are in the tombs will hear [the voice of the Son of God] and will come out, those who have done good deeds to the resurrection of life, but those who have done wicked deeds to the resurrection of condemnation." (Jn 5: 28-29)

MONDAY

So Jesus, perturbed again, came to the tomb. It was a cave, and a stone lay across it. Jesus said, "Take away the stone." (Jn 11: 38-39a)

TUESDAY

When [Jesus] got out of the boat, at once a man from the tombs who had an unclean spirit met him. The man had been dwelling among the tombs. Night and day among the tombs [...] he was always crying out. (Mk 5: 2-3a, 5)

WEDNESDAY

Anyone can see that the wisest die,/ the fool and the senseless pass away too./ Tombs are their homes for ever./ This is the destiny of those who trust in folly. (Ps 49: 11a, 12a, 14a)

THURSDAY

The earth quaked, rocks were split, tombs were opened, and the bodies of many saints who had fallen asleep were raised. And coming forth from their tombs after his resurrection, they entered the holy city and appeared to many. (Mt 27: 51b-53)

Friday

"Woe to you! You are like unseen graves over which people unknowingly walk." (Lk 11: 44)

Saturday

Then they went away quickly from the tomb, fearful yet overjoyed, and ran to announce this to his disciples. (Mt 28: 8)

LITANY BEFORE CHRIST'S TOMB

℟ Lord, be our life!

‣ Your tomb is a tabernacle; make my life a vigil of adoration. ℟

‣ Bless the expectation of hope with which I approach your tomb. ℟

‣ May the wonder of your tomb let me see beyond the limits I impose on my life. ℟

‣ I consign to your tomb all my powerlessness and whatever makes me want to give up. ℟

‣ May the power of your unseen presence free me from all the absence that saddens my life. ℟

‣ At your tomb make of my life a new beginning. ℟

‣ When disappointment and despair keep me from confronting your tomb: ℟

‣ Help me to face whatever in me needs to die. ℟

‣ May the sign of hope of your tomb accompany me in all life's difficulties. ℟

‣ By drawing close to you in death may I know your intimacy in my life. ℟

‣ I leave at your tomb all my discouragement, my despondency, and defeat. ℟

‹ At your tomb put asunder all my false hopes, negativity, and pessimism. ℟

‹ United with you in your tomb, liberate me from all self-reliance and self-assertion. ℟

‹ Let me see every mark of death in my life as the occasion for the Father to manifest his life-giving power. ℟

‹ May your tomb convert me from the temptation to build monuments to self-importance and self-glory. ℟

‹ May your open tomb free me from whatever keeps me closed in on myself. ℟

‹ There is nothing closed that you cannot open; help me look beyond the impossible. ℟

‹ Roll away the stone of resistance and rebellion in my life. ℟

‹ Roll away the stone of anger and resentment. ℟

‹ Roll away my indifference and lethargy. ℟

‹ Roll away the stone of bitterness and regret. ℟

‹ Roll away the stone of individualism and alienation. ℟

‹ Roll away the stone of skepticism that makes me doubtful of your promises. ℟

‹ May my generosity and mercy match the wideness of your open tomb. ℟

‹ Empty me of every false ambition and aspiration like your empty tomb. ℟

‹ May the suppleness of your tomb break down all the defenses I set up. ℟

‹ May the openness of your tomb soften my stony heart. ℟

‹ May the wonder of your tomb recharge my life with freedom. ℟

‹ May the emptiness of your tomb reassure me of your unfailing presence. ℟

Blessing of the
Resurrection

Word of God
1 Peter 1: 3-5

BLESSED BE THE GOD and Father of our Lord Jesus Christ, who in his great mercy gave us a new birth to a living hope through the resurrection of Jesus Christ from the dead, to an inheritance that is imperishable, undefiled, and unfading, kept in heaven for you who by the power of God are safeguarded through faith, to a salvation that is ready to be revealed in the final time.

LITANY OF RESURRECTION GRACES

℟ **Risen Savior, stay with me.**

‣ Lord Jesus, by your Resurrection you have reconciled all people to God. ℟

‣ Lord Jesus, when you rose from the dead you blessed us with the Easter gift of peace. ℟

‣ Lord Jesus, by your rising you restored us to friendship with the Father. ℟

‣ Lord Jesus, on the seashore you cooked breakfast for your disciples. ℟

‣ Lord Jesus, you invite us to touch your wounds and to throw off all doubt. ℟

‣ Lord Jesus, you returned us to God's favor and intimacy when we were rebellious and estranged. ℟

‣ Lord Jesus, by your Death and Resurrection you have forgiven our sins. ℟

‣ Lord Jesus, you have made satisfaction for our iniquity. ℟

◂ Lord Jesus, you have redeemed us and given us freedom from sin, from death, and from self. ℟

◂ Lord Jesus, you have justified us and made us upright before the Father. ℟

◂ Lord Jesus, your Resurrection has liberated us from all fatalism, negativity, and dread. ℟

◂ Lord Jesus, your Resurrection endows us with the confidence and the certainty of the apostles. ℟

◂ Lord Jesus, you endow us with the wisdom and courage to live the Truth. ℟

◂ Lord Jesus, by your Resurrection you have formed your people into the communion of the Church. ℟

◂ Lord Jesus, your Resurrection assures us that your mercy is offered to us at every moment as a new beginning. ℟

◂ Lord Jesus, in your Resurrection is the hope of our own resurrection. ℟

Blessing for
Mary's Maternal Mediation

The month of May is a graced time to call to mind the mysteries of the Blessed Virgin Mary and to enter into them through our devout reliance on the mediation of the Mother of God. The individual prayers for each day might begin with the Hail Mary and end with the concluding prayer that is provided or with some other Marian prayer, such as the Memorare *or the Hail Holy* Queen. *Various members of the family can share the different parts of the blessing.*

Sunday: The Immaculate Conception

O Mary Immaculate, your unique perfection, which is the fruit of the Father's goodness, reveals the sanctity to which every child of God is called. May your Immaculate Conception save me from all worldly deception. May the miracle of your creation convince me that with God all things are possible. Break through the darkness of my life even as God broke through the stranglehold of sin when you were conceived. Help me to live in hope by depending on your love as the way to recover the innocence of Eden and to reach my eternal destiny, your Son Jesus Christ.

Monday: The Annunciation

O Mary, full of grace, the Annunciation is the beginning of our salvation. By your holy *Fiat*, the earth has become heaven. For God has placed in the midst of our barren and despairing world a new beginning who is your little Boy. All my desires, my deepest longings, all that my heart cries out for became Flesh in your womb. Conform me to your graced obedience. May my praying the Hail Mary cause the Word of God to germinate in my soul and to bear the Fruit of Life, your divine Son. May every aspect of my life announce the saving presence of Jesus Christ for all the world to encounter.

TUESDAY: The Visitation

O Blessed Virgin, you never fail to come into my life bearing in your womb Jesus your Son. Elizabeth was expecting the birth of the impossible. But the divine Presence whom you carried to your cousin convinced her to expect even *more*. Make my life one of unending welcome. Help me to see that holiness means receiving the grace God sends me through you. Your Visitation is the way that I stay in front of the mystery who is Jesus Christ, so to live in the Truth. In your coming I rejoice with the joy that enables me to look with love at every presence filled with passion for Christ.

WEDNESDAY: The Nativity

O most holy Mother of God, from the moment of the Christmas miracle your blessed womb remains ever fruitful, for it is you who are our Mother. How we rely on your incomparable merits and your maternal intercession for our spiritual birth and our growth in the life of grace. You are the *Theotokos*, not only because you conceived and gave birth to the Son of God, but also because you accompanied Jesus in his human growth. Accompany us as well with your motherly tenderness. Everything you touch becomes human. Make us more human with the humanity of your Son.

THURSDAY: The Wedding at Cana

O Mother of Jesus, at the wedding feast of Cana you revealed how you concern yourself with even the most meager human needs. No problem or suffering escapes your motherly gaze. Your solicitude makes me certain that your Son, the true Bridegroom, longs to intervene in the most menial moments of my life. The miraculous wine of Cana, that foreshadows the Precious Blood, slakes my aching thirst for God. O Mary, Fountain of Hope, lead me anew to Jesus, the Fountain of Holiness. Keep me close to you so that I will be always generous and responsive to do whatever Jesus tells me.

FRIDAY: Our Lady of Sorrows

Most Sorrowful Mother, as he died on the cross, your beloved Son commanded us to behold you as our Mother. From the first moment of your existence you led us to your Son. But even in his dying, Jesus leads us to you. For we need your maternal purity to sustain us when overcome by the terrifying darkness of faith. Your sharing in the cross of your Son makes that event more deeply human, and fills me with confidence to face the sufferings and horrors of life. Our Lady of Compassion, help me to obey your Son and to behold you with fortitude and confidence as I take up the cross.

SATURDAY: The Assumption

O Mary, Queen of Heaven, you reign in paradise, body and soul, as a sublime sign of hope for the whole human race. Thank you for the gift of your motherly protection that remains for ever the living icon of the Father's mercy. Through the mystery of your elevation, uplift my heart and help me to keep my thoughts on heaven. Through your unique intercession, bless me with the capacity to await God's future and to abandon myself to the Lord's promises. Fill me with strength, purity, resoluteness, trust, and peace. May my days be filled with the same joy that you bring to the angels in heaven.

May Blessing for
Marian Graces

"I was greatly helped by a book by Saint Louis Marie Grignion de Montfort entitled *Treatise of True Devotion to the Blessed Virgin*. There I found the answers to my questions. Yes, Mary does bring us closer to Christ; she does lead us to him, provided that we live her mystery in Christ... And so, thanks to Saint Louis, I began to discover the immense riches of Marian devotion from new perspectives."

Blessed John Paul II

Word of God

Sunday

Mary said, "Behold, I am the handmaid of the Lord. May it be done to me according to your word." (Lk 1: 38)

Monday

And Mary said: "My soul proclaims the greatness of the Lord;/ my spirit rejoices in God my savior." (Lk 1: 46-47)

Tuesday

So [the shepherds] went in haste and found Mary and Joseph, and the infant lying in the manger. And Mary kept all these things, reflecting on them in her heart. (Lk 2: 16, 19)

Wednesday

Simeon blessed them and said to Mary his mother, "You yourself a sword will pierce so that the thoughts of many hearts may be revealed." (Lk 2: 34a, 35)

THURSDAY

[Jesus'] mother said to the servers, "Do whatever he tells you." (Jn 2: 5)

FRIDAY

[Jesus] said to the disciple, "Behold, your mother." And from that hour the disciple took [Mary] into his home. (Jn 19: 27)

SATURDAY

They went to the upper room where they were staying. All these devoted themselves with one accord to prayer, together with some women, and Mary the mother of Jesus. (Acts 1: 13a, 14)

LITANY
(Based on Saint Louis Marie Grignion de Montfort's book *Treatise of True Devotion to the Blessed Virgin*)

℟ **Mary, may we live your mystery in Christ.**

‹ God deigned to perfect his greatest designs through the most Blessed Virgin. ℟

‹ Through Mary alone God gave his only-begotten Son to the world. ℟

‹ The Father gave his Son to Mary so that the world would receive him through her. ℟

‹ God communicated to Mary his own fecundity so that she might bring forth the members of his mystical Body. ℟

‹ God-made-Man found his freedom in being shut within Mary's womb. ℟

‹ The more the Holy Spirit finds Mary in a soul, the more powerfully he works to produce Jesus Christ in that soul. ℟

‹ God made a gathering of all graces and called it Mary. ℟

◖ It is through Mary that Jesus applies his merits, communicates his virtues, and distributes his graces. ℟

◖ Mary is the mysterious channel by which Christ pours forth his mercies. ℟

◖ God has designed that we should have all things in Mary. ℟

◖ God the Son desires to be formed and incarnated daily through his Mother. ℟

◖ It is Mary alone who has found grace before God without the aid of another mere creature. ℟

◖ Whoever finds Mary shall find Jesus Christ, the Way, the Truth, and the Life. ℟

◖ Mary's purpose is to unite us with Jesus Christ, her Son. ℟

◖ It is the wish of her Son that we should come to him through his Blessed Mother. ℟

◖ Seeing Mary, we see our own human nature. ℟

◖ We come to Mary as to the way which leads directly to Jesus. ℟

◖ The truly devout live by the faith of Jesus and Mary, and not by natural emotions and feelings. ℟

◖ We do not love the Blessed Virgin because of what we obtain; we love her because she is worthy of our love. ℟

◖ The more we are consecrated to Mary, the more perfectly are we united with Jesus Christ. ℟

◖ Seeing that we are unworthy, God gives graces to Mary so that through her we may receive all that he wishes to give us. ℟

◖ Through Mary's mediation our Lord receives the glory and the gratitude that we owe him. ℟

◖ Mary purifies all our good works from every stain of self-love and false attachment. ℟

‹ We will never bear heavy crosses joyfully and with perseverance unless we have a tender devotion to the Blessed Virgin. ℟

‹ Devotion to the Blessed Virgin is the perfect way to reach Jesus Christ and to unite ourselves with him. ℟

‹ No one is filled with the living thought of God except through Mary. ℟

‹ The frequent thought and loving invocation of Mary is a sure indication that a soul is not estranged from God. ℟

‹ We trust in Mary's fidelity, we lean on her strength, we build upon her mercy and charity in order that she may preserve and increase our virtues. ℟

‹ The Mother of fair love removes from our hearts all scruples and every taint of slavish and disordered fear. ℟

‹ Mary opens our heart and makes it big and generous. ℟

‹ The Blessed Virgin will fill us with great confidence in God and in herself. ℟

‹ Mary is the mold designed to form and shape God-like creatures. ℟

‹ The Hail Mary devoutly said causes the Word of God to germinate in our souls. ℟

‹ To be led by the spirit of Mary, we must renounce our own spirit. ℟

‹ Let us cast ourselves down with a profound sense of our own nothingness in the presence of Jesus living in Mary. ℟

‹ Whoever desires to have the fruit of life, Jesus Christ, must have the tree of life, which is Mary. ℟

Blessing to
Prepare for Pentecost

WORD OF GOD

*"To each individual the manifestation of the Spirit
is given for some benefit."
(1 Cor 12: 7)*

*BLESSING OF THE MANIFESTATION
OF THE HOLY SPIRIT*

℟ **Come, Holy Spirit. Or:** *Veni, Sancte Spiritus.*

◄ "Before the Holy Spirit came, the humanity of Christ, to which human affection clung, needed to be taken away from before the eyes of the disciples. We were not able to receive both Jesus and the Holy Spirit, and neither could we endure the presence of both." (Saint Augustine) ℟

◄ "The Holy Spirit, finding us in a state of deformity, restores our original beauty and fills us with his grace, leaving no room for anything unworthy of his love." (Didymus of Alexandria) ℟

◄ "The presence of the gift of the Holy Spirit is the fuller the greater a person's desire to be worthy of it." (Saint Hilary) ℟

◄ "Only the Holy Spirit can purify the intellect, for unless a greater power comes and overthrows the despoiler, what he has taken captive will never be set free." (Saint Diadochos of Photiki) ℟

◄ "No one can ever attain to the remedy of forgiveness who does not have the Paraclete to intercede for him. For it is through him we call upon the Father; from him come the tears of repentance, from him the groans of those who kneel in supplication." (Saint Leo the Great) ℞

‹ "The fire of the Holy Spirit, like a refining fire with gold, makes what is good better, and devours sin as stubble." (Saint Ambrose) ℞

‹ "See how the Holy Spirit wipes away all this iniquity, and uplifts to the highest dignity those who before had been betrayed by their own sins." (Saint John Chrysostom) ℞

‹ "The Holy Spirit comes gently. He is not felt as a burden. The Spirit comes with the tenderness of a true friend and protector to save, to heal, to teach, to counsel, to strengthen, to console. The Holy Spirit enables us to see things beyond the range of human vision." (Saint Cyril of Jerusalem) ℞

‹ "The Holy Spirit interiorly perfects our spirit, communicating to it a new dynamism so that it refrains from evil for love… In this way it is free – not in the sense that it is not subject to the divine law; it is free because its interior dynamism makes it do what divine law prescribes." (Saint Thomas Aquinas) ℞

‹ "Fittingly did the Holy Spirit appear in fire because in every heart that he enters into he drives out the torpor of coldness, and kindles there the desire of his own eternity. As the Spirit touches a soul, he teaches it. The human spirit suddenly changes; it rejects on the instant what it was, and shows itself at once as it was not." (Saint Gregory the Great) ℞

‹ "With the Holy Spirit within them it is quite natural for people who had been absorbed by the things of this world to become entirely other-worldly in outlook, and for cowards to become people of great courage." (Saint Cyril of Alexandria) ℞

‹ "Through the Holy Spirit we acquire a likeness to God; indeed, we attain what is beyond our most sublime aspirations – we become God." (Saint Basil) ℞

Blessing of the
Sacred Heart

"The Sacred Heart [is] a 'refuge' in which to recover, the seat of mercy, the encounter with him who is the source of the Lord's infinite love, the fount from which flows the Holy Spirit, the promised land, and true paradise."

Directory on Popular Piety and the Liturgy, 169

WORD OF GOD

SUNDAY

"Where your treasure is, there also will your heart be." (Mt 6: 21)

MONDAY

At the sight of the crowds, [Jesus'] heart was moved with pity for them because they were troubled and abandoned, like sheep without a shepherd. (Mt 9: 36)

TUESDAY

"Take my yoke upon you and learn from me, for I am meek and humble of heart; and you will find rest for yourselves." (Mt 11: 29)

WEDNESDAY

When [Jesus] disembarked and saw the vast crowd, his heart was moved with pity for them, and he cured their sick. (Mt 14: 14)

THURSDAY

Jesus summoned his disciples and said, "My heart is moved with pity for the crowd, for they have been with me now for three days and have nothing to eat. I do not want to send them away hungry, for fear they may collapse on the way." (Mt 15: 32)

FRIDAY

[Jesus] said to [the scholar of the law], "You shall love the Lord, your God, with all your heart, with all your soul, and with all your mind." (Mt 22: 37)

SATURDAY

My sacrifice, God, is a broken spirit;/ God, do not spurn a broken, humbled heart. (Ps 51: 19)

LITANY OF THE SACRED HEART
(Based on *Haurietis Aquas*, the encyclical on the Sacred Heart by Pope Pius XII)

℟ **Lord Jesus, give me your Heart.**

‹ The Heart of the divine Redeemer is the natural sign and symbol of his boundless love for the human race. ℟

‹ In the Sacred Heart is the express image of the infinite love of Jesus Christ which moves us to love in return. ℟

‹ The Heart of the incarnate Word is a symbol of that divine love which the Redeemer shares with the Father and the Holy Spirit. ℟

‹ The Heart of the incarnate Word is the symbol of that burning love which enriches the human will of Christ and enlightens and governs its acts. ℟

‹ The Heart of the incarnate Word is the symbol of sensible love since the body of Jesus Christ possesses full powers of feeling and perception. ℟

‹ We ought to meditate most lovingly on the beating of Christ's Sacred Heart by which he seemed to measure the time of his sojourn on earth. ℟

◦ We can enter into the secret places of this divine Heart and gaze at the abundant riches of God's grace. ℟

◦ The adorable Heart of Jesus Christ began to beat with a love at once human and divine after the Virgin Mary generously pronounced her *Fiat*. ℟

◦ By learning the heart of God in the words of God, we long more ardently for things eternal. ℟

◦ The divine Redeemer hanging on the cross showed that his Heart was strongly moved by different emotions – burning love, desolation, pity, longing, desire, unruffled peace. ℟

◦ The divine Eucharist and the priesthood are gifts of the Sacred Heart of Jesus. ℟

◦ Another most precious gift of the Lord's Sacred Heart is Mary the beloved Mother of God and the most loving Mother of us all. ℟

◦ From the wounded Heart of the Redeemer was born the Church, the dispenser of the Blood of the Redemption. ℟

◦ The Redeemer pours forth grace from his pierced Heart. ℟

◦ After our Lord had ascended into heaven he did not cease to remain with the Church by means of the burning love with which his Heart beats. ℟

◦ The Lord keeps in his Heart, locked as it were in a most precious shrine, the unlimited treasures of his merits. ℟

◦ The infusion of divine charity had its origin in the Heart of the Savior. ℟

◦ The clearest image of the all-embracing fullness of God is the Heart of Christ Jesus itself. ℟

‹ From something corporeal such as the Heart of Jesus Christ it is fitting for us to mount to a consideration and adoration of the infused heavenly love. ℟

‹ The honor to be paid to the Sacred Heart is such as to raise it to the rank of the highest expression of Christian piety. ℟

‹ We cannot reach the Heart of God save through the Heart of Christ. ℟

‹ In paying homage to the Sacred Heart, Christians surrender themselves to their Redeemer with regard to both the affections of the heart and the external activities of their life. ℟

‹ Through devotion to the Sacred Heart, the faithful have the firm conviction that they are moved to honor God for the sake of God's goodness. ℟

‹ Devotion to the Sacred Heart of Jesus is the most effective school of the love of God. ℟

‹ In the Sacred Heart of Jesus must all our hopes be placed. ℟

Blessing for the
Graces of
Saints Peter and Paul

"In Peter the weak things of the world were chosen, to confound the strong; in Paul sin abounded so that grace might abound the more. In each of them what shone forth was the great grace and glory of God, who made them deserving."

Saint Augustine

| Word of God | 1 Peter 2: 10, 19, 24 |

Y OU "HAD NOT received mercy"/ but now you have received mercy. Whenever anyone bears the pain of unjust suffering because of consciousness of God, that is a grace. By [Christ's] wounds you have been healed.

| Word of God | 2 Corinthians 1: 9 |

I NDEED, we had accepted within ourselves the sentence of death, that we might trust not in ourselves but in God who raises the dead.

MEDITATION

"The miracles of Peter and Paul show what sinners can do who have submitted to the service that God has commanded. What our Lord thought of his holy Mother and Saint John the Baptist and of John the Disciple, our minds cannot conceive, but what he thought of repentant sinners, or in other words, men who served him earnestly, we know. He loved them, and filled them with the Holy Spirit. They slept while he suffered, they thrust forward the evil motives of corrupt wills as he preached, they quailed in his resurrected presence like dogs, they clung to his high principles only by tortured effort, they knew and preached him yet wallowed in temptations, but he desired to be with them with a brother's love, and to become part of their flesh in order to raise them up for ever. Shall we doubt their capacities, after this? Is it to be supposed that Christ loved in this way an ineradicable and impotent wickedness, never to be separated from souls; or shall we believe that he loved souls because they can so quickly become his brothers?"

Rose Hawthorne Lathrop (Mother Alphonsa)

LITANY TO OBTAIN THE GRACES OF SAINTS PETER AND PAUL

GLORIOUS SAINT PETER:

‣ The Lord Jesus saw you and called you to be his Fisherman:
– may I always be responsive and obedient to Christ in my vocation.

‣ You knelt before the Lord asking him to leave you when you saw the miraculous catch of fish:
– may I be always receptive to the signs of Christ's love and open to his presence.

‣ You declared Jesus to be the Messiah, the Son of the living God:
– may I always live your certainty and faith in Jesus Christ.

‣ You are the one whom the Lord named "Rock":
– may I remain always united to the Church and eager for her absolution for my sins.

‣ You witnessed the Transfiguration of our Lord:
– may I always keep before me your delight in the radiance and beauty of Christ.

‣ You asked the Lord how many times we are to forgive our wrongdoers:
– may I always be lavish in showing God's mercy to others.

⁌ You tried to stop our Lord from washing your feet:
– may I never resist the unexpected ways that Christ offers to draw me close to himself.

⁌ You fell asleep in the garden when our Lord was in agony:
– may I be always attentive and alert to the action of Christ in my life even in my fragility.

⁌ You went out and wept bitterly after you denied Jesus three times:
– may I never be without trust and confidence in God's mercy whenever I am faced by the horror of my own misery and sins.

⁌ You ran with the apostle John to the tomb of Jesus:
– may your hope, conviction, and expectation reign always in my heart.

⁌ You confessed to the risen Jesus three times that you love him:
– may I always be quick in claiming Christ's love, even when I know that there is nothing in me to make me worthy of it.

⁌ You preached and in one day three thousand people were converted to the faith:
– may I listen to the Word, love the Church, and live as a missionary of the Gospel.

GLORIOUS SAINT PAUL:

⁌ The Lord Jesus called you on the road to Damascus and asked why you were persecuting him:
– help me to overcome all my obstinacy and my defiance of God's will.

⁌ You are the instrument Christ Jesus chose to bring his name to the Gentiles:
– may I always cooperate with the way God wants to use me for his glory.

⁌ You preached in the Areopagus to those who worshiped "A God Unknown":

– by your intercession, may I lead others to union with Christ whom they long for in their hearts.

‹ You were a true father to those whom you begot in Christ Jesus through your preaching of the Gospel:
– may I always depend on your paternal solicitude and care.

‹ You were scourged, stoned, shipwrecked, and imprisoned:
– help me to place all my confidence in Christ when faced by great suffering.

‹ You begged the Lord three times to remove the thorn in your flesh:
– may I always live in complete abandonment to the grace of Jesus in my life.

‹ You declared that you were content with weakness, mistreatment, distress, persecutions, and difficulties for the sake of Christ:
– may I always live the truth that when I am powerless it is then that I am strong.

‹ You taught us that love is patient, love is kind:
– may I always live your witness of authentic Christian love.

‹ You taught us that we have received a spirit of adoption through which we cry out, "*Abba*, Father!":
– may I always live according to the law of the spirit.

‹ You moved us to offer our bodies as a living sacrifice to God:
– may I never conform myself to this age but be transformed by the renewal of my mind.

‹ The Church in Miletus wept when you departed from them:
– may I always love you tenderly as teacher, missionary, companion, and apostle.

‹ You instructed us to imitate you as you imitate Christ:
– may I always embrace your example of total self-donation, courage, and passion for Christ.

Blessing of
Saint Paul

"It was precisely on the road to Damascus… that, according to Paul's words, 'Christ made me his own' (Phil 3: 12)… Paul goes directly to the essential and speaks… above all of a revelation and of a vocation in the encounter with the Risen One… His conversion was… the result… of divine intervention, an unforeseeable, divine grace… What counts is to place Jesus Christ at the center of our lives, so that our identity is marked essentially by the encounter, by communion with Christ and with his Word."

Pope Benedict XVI

Saint Paul understood clearly that his conversion to Christianity would be for the good of others as well as for his own good. In one of his letters, Saint Paul explains that "Christ Jesus came into the world to save sinners. Of these I am the foremost. But for that reason I was mercifully treated, so that in me, as the foremost, Christ Jesus might display all his patience as an example for those who would come to believe in him for everlasting life" (1 Tm 1: 15-16). It is therefore fitting for us to meditate on the life of Saint Paul. As we pray this blessing, we follow the holy example of the Apostle in the hopes of deepening our belief in Christ Jesus by becoming sharers in the powerful graces that so transformed Saint Paul's life.

Opening Prayer

Glorious Apostle Paul, help me at the beginning of this new day to offer my body and the whole of my life as a living sacrifice to God. Do not permit me to conform myself to this age but rather, by your intercession, may I be transformed by the renewal of my mind. Through this renewal help me to judge what is God's will, what is good, pleasing, and perfect. For the one whom I seek and serve is Jesus Christ who is the Lord, now and for ever.

WORD OF GOD

SUNDAY

When the kindness and generous love/ of God our savior appeared,/ not because of any righteous deeds we had done/ but because of his mercy,/ he saved us through the bath of rebirth/ and renewal by the holy Spirit,/ whom he richly poured out on us/ through Jesus Christ our savior. (Ti 3: 4-6)

MONDAY

You have had yourselves washed, you were sanctified, you were justified in the name of the Lord Jesus Christ and in the Spirit of our God. (1 Cor 6: 11)

TUESDAY

I rejoice in my sufferings for your sake, and in my flesh I am filling up what is lacking in the afflictions of Christ on behalf of his body, which is the church. (Col 1: 24)

WEDNESDAY

You did not receive a spirit of slavery to fall back into fear, but you received a spirit of adoption, through which we cry, "*Abba*, Father!" The Spirit itself bears witness with our spirit that we are children of God. (Rom 8: 15-16)

THURSDAY

A thorn in the flesh was given to me. Three times I begged the Lord about this, that it might leave me, but he said to me, "My grace is sufficient for you, for power is made perfect in weakness." I will rather boast most gladly of my weaknesses, in order that the power of Christ may dwell with me. (2 Cor 12: 7, 8-9)

FRIDAY

I have been crucified with Christ; yet I live, no longer I, but Christ lives in me; insofar as I now live in the flesh, I live by faith in the Son of God who has loved me and given himself up for me. (Gal 2: 19b-20)

SATURDAY

To me life is Christ, and death is gain. (Phil 1: 21)

LITANY OF THE GRACES OF SAINT PAUL

℟ **For me to live is Christ.**

GLORIOUS SAINT PAUL:

‣ **You concurred in the stoning of Stephen:**
– help me to recognize how God uses even my sin to draw me closer to him and to perfect me in his love. ℟

‣ **The Lord Jesus delivered you and sent you to open the eyes of others so as to turn them from darkness to light and from the power of Satan to God:**
– pray that I may be freed from all evil and be given forgiveness for my sins. ℟

‣ **After encountering Jesus on the road to Damascus, you were blind for three days:**
– help me to realize that in the dark moments of my life God is preparing me for greater things. ℟

‣ **The Lord revealed to Ananias how much you would have to suffer for the name of Jesus as his instrument:**
– help me to accept the suffering present in my life as a way of serving God and living for Christ. ℟

‣ **Ananias told you that God had designated you to know his will, to see the Righteous One, and to hear the sound of his voice:**
– please intercede that I may have some share in your grace of holiness. ℟

◄ When your enemies conspired to kill you, fellow Christians helped you to escape from the city by lowering you down the wall in a basket:
– help me to confide myself to the unfailing care of Jesus Christ especially as I find it in the companions you give me. ℟

◄ While you were fasting and praying, the Holy Spirit revealed a mission God had in store for you:
– help me to be docile and attentive to all the ways that the Holy Spirit wants to speak to me and use me. ℟

◄ The Lord made you a light to the nations and a means of salvation to the ends of the earth:
– help me to be obedient to God's will and committed to evangelization. ℟

◄ When you were stoned by the people in Lystra, your disciples prayed in a circle around you until you arose and walked back into the town:
– help me to pray unceasingly and to have the courage to face the persecution that is part of being a Christian. ℟

◄ At Cenchreae you shaved your head because of a vow you had taken:
– help me to be resolute and true in my "yes" of faith to Jesus Christ. ℟

◄ When the people at Miletus wept when they heard that they would never see your face again, you commended them to the gracious Word of God:
– help me to embrace the presence of God when life's problems leave me feeling helpless or alone. ℟

◄ When the ship that bore you to your trial in Rome was on the verge of shipwreck and the sailors were despairing, you assured them that they would not lose even a hair of their heads:
– help me to meet the devastating circumstances of my life with a hope that is steadfast, certain, and firm. ℟

‹ When you were shipwrecked in Malta, you were bitten by a poisonous snake, yet you suffered no harm:
– help be to be free from fear even before those things that terrify me the most. ℞

‹ During your two-year imprisonment in Rome you preached the reign of God and taught about the Lord Jesus Christ:
– help me to realize that every situation of my life is an opportunity to witness to my faith, to love Jesus Christ, and to glorify God. ℞

‹ When you begged the Lord to remove the thorn in your flesh, you accepted that Christ's grace was enough for you:
– help me always to rely on the grace of Christ and not on my own resources, especially when my trials seem oppressive. ℞

‹ You asked the Romans in the letter you wrote to them if they realized that God's kindness was an invitation to them to repent:
– help me to acknowledge God's love and kindness in my life through my fervent and renewed repentance. ℞

‹ You have assured us that we have received a spirit of adoption that moves us to cry out "*Abba*, Father!":
– help me to live according to the Spirit as a true child of God in unwavering confidence, fidelity, love, and trust. ℞

CLOSING PRAYER

LOVING FATHER, from time immemorial you designated the Apostle Paul to know your will, to look upon the Just One, and to hear the sound of his voice. Paul's love for your Son was beyond all telling. For Christ emptied himself and took the form of a slave, obediently accepting even death on a cross. Paul followed Jesus in this path of humility and total self-giving. Help me to imitate Paul as Paul imitated Christ. May my life, in all that I think, say, and do, proclaim to your eternal glory that Jesus Christ is Lord.

A Blessing to
Share in the Graces
of the Transfiguration

WORD OF GOD

SUNDAY

While [Jesus] was praying his face changed in appearance and his clothing became dazzling white. (Lk 9: 29)

MONDAY

We did not follow cleverly devised myths when we made known to you the power and coming of our Lord Jesus Christ, but we had been eyewitnesses of his majesty. For he received honor and glory from God the Father when that unique declaration came to him from the majestic glory, "This is my Son, my beloved, with whom I am well pleased." We ourselves heard this voice come from heaven while we were with him on the holy mountain. (2 Pt 1: 16-18)

TUESDAY

My being thirsts for God, the living God./ When can I go and see the face of God? (Ps 42: 3)

WEDNESDAY

Let your face shine on your servant;/ save me in your kindness. (Ps 31: 17)

THURSDAY

All those who sat in the Sanhedrin looked intently at [Stephen] and saw that his face was like the face of an angel. (Acts 6: 15)

FRIDAY

For God who said, "Let light shine out of darkness," has shone in our hearts to bring to light the knowledge of the glory of God on the face of [Jesus] Christ. (2 Cor 4: 6)

SATURDAY

All of us, gazing with unveiled face on the glory of the Lord, are being transformed into the same image from glory to glory, as from the Lord who is the Spirit. (2 Cor 3: 18)

LITANY OF THE TRANSFIGURATION

℟ **Let me see only Jesus.**

❧ When I'm tempted to look at only my faults: ℟

❧ When troubled by the specter of doubt and defeat: ℟

❧ When I can't see beyond the frustrations of the moment: ℟

❧ When the horizon seems distant and dark: ℟

❧ When I can't see the point of pursuing what's good: ℟

❧ When complaining and cynicism invade my peace: ℟

❧ When I can't face my problems: ℟

❧ When the world looks bleak: ℟

❧ When others measure and judge me: ℟

❧ When beset by depression: ℟

❧ When friendship is far from me: ℟

❧ When overshadowed by sorrow: ℟

❧ When I fail to use my freedom: ℟

❧ When it's hard to forgive: ℟

‹ When things don't make sense: ℟

‹ When I think I can't change: ℟

‹ When confronted by suffering: ℟

‹ When stress gets me down: ℟

‹ When it's hard to go on: ℟

‹ When blinded by sin: ℟

‹ When the hardness of life overwhelms me: ℟

‹ When hope begins to fade: ℟

Closing Prayer

LOVING FATHER, thank you for allowing me to witness the vision of your Son transfigured on Mount Tabor. May I become what I behold so that my life will radiate the glory and grace that remain your priceless gifts to me in Jesus.

Blessing to
Exalt the Cross of Christ

Then [Jesus] said to all, "If anyone wishes to come after me, he must deny himself and take up his cross daily and follow me." (Lk 9: 23)

WORD OF GOD

SUNDAY

The message of the cross is foolishness to those who are perishing, but to us who are being saved it is the power of God. (1 Cor 1: 18)

MONDAY

May I never boast except in the cross of our Lord Jesus Christ, through which the world has been crucified to me, and I to the world. (Gal 6: 14)

TUESDAY

[Christ] abolish[ed] the law with its commandments and legal claims, that he might create in himself one new person in place of the two, thus establishing peace, and might reconcile both with God, in one body, through the cross, putting that enmity to death by it. (Eph 2: 15-16)

WEDNESDAY

For many, as I have often told you and now tell you even in tears, conduct themselves as enemies of the cross of Christ. (Phil 3: 18)

THURSDAY

For in him all the fullness was pleased to dwell,/ and through him to reconcile all things for him,/ making peace by the blood of his cross/ [through him], whether those on earth or those in heaven. He brought you to life along with him, having forgiven us all our transgressions; obliterating the bond against us, with its legal claims, which was opposed to us, he also removed it from our midst, nailing it to the cross. (Col 1: 19-20; 2: 13b-14)

FRIDAY

For the sake of the joy that lay before him [Jesus] endured the cross, despising its shame, and has taken his seat at the right of the throne of God. (Heb 12: 2)

SATURDAY

[Christ] himself bore our sins in his body upon the cross, so that, free from sin, we might live for righteousness. By his wounds you have been healed. (1 Pt 2: 24)

LITANY TO HAIL THE CROSS

℟ **Hail, O Cross, our only hope! Or: *Ave Crux, Spes Unica!***

‹ **Saint Anselm:** "O Holy Cross, by you hell is despoiled, by you its mouth is stopped up to all the redeemed. By you demons are made afraid and restrained, conquered, and trampled underfoot. By you the world is renewed and made beautiful with truth." ℟

‹ **From a Medieval Litany:** "O Holy Cross, guide of the blind, way of those who have gone astray, staff of the lame, consolation of the poor, succor of the distressed, hope of the hopeless, rampart of the besieged, rest of the afflicted, knowledge of the ignorant, sure rule of life, clothing of the naked." ℟

‹ **Saint Paulinus of Nola:** "O Cross, by your means, man in God is crowned king in heaven. You gave believers power to make the pantheon of the nations quake; you are the soul of peace that unites men in Christ the mediator. Be always for us, your faithful, both pillar and anchor; watch over our homes, set the course of our ship." ℟

‹ Venantius Fortunatus: "O blessed Tree, that with your arms/ support the Savior of the world/ a balance for that flesh divine/ that snatched away the prey of hell./ Hail Cross, our one and only hope,/ in this our time of mourning, grant/ that all the faithful grow in grace/ and sinners have their guilt forgiven." ℟

‹ Girolamo Savonarola: "Cross of torture! May'st thou rend me/ With thy fierce, unearthly dole;/ Welcome be the pangs that lend me/ Strength to crush sin in my soul./ Then in glory, parted never/ From the blessed Savior's side,/ Graven on my heart for ever/ Be the Cross, and Crucified." ℟

‹ Byzantine Liturgy: "O Cross of the Lord, through you the dismay of tears has passed away, and we have been saved from the snares of death and carried up into imperishable joy. You have procured for us the enjoyment of everlasting glory. O life-bearing Cross, Door of Paradise, Strength of Believers, Wall of the Church, through which decay has disappeared and perished: truly, you are the Haven of Salvation that grants great mercy to the world." ℟

‹ Saint Theodorus the Studite: "Cross of Christ, protect those who with burning hearts sing to you; protect those who with faithful spirit kiss and embrace you; govern your subjects in peace and true faith." ℟

‹ Blessed John Paul II: "We hail you, O Holy Cross! You bring us the One who twenty centuries ago was acclaimed in Jerusalem by the crowd: 'Blessed is he who comes in the name of the Lord.'" ℟

Blessing to
Benefit from the Graces of the Rosary

"When in the rosary we plead with Mary the sanctuary of the Holy Spirit (see Lk 1: 35), she intercedes for us before the Father, who filled her with grace, and before the Son born of her womb, praying with us and for us."

Blessed John Paul II

In his apostolic letter on the rosary entitled Rosarium Virginis Mariae, *Blessed John Paul II writes: "The Rosary does indeed mark the rhythm of human life, bringing it into harmony with the rhythm of God's own life, in the joyful communion of the Holy Trinity, our life's destiny and deepest longing" (25). As a way of responding to the yearning for that harmony in our own lives, this blessing is a litany based on the Holy Father's apostolic letter.*

LITANY OF ROSARY GRACES

℟ **Queen of the rosary, turn your eyes of mercy toward us.**

Most merciful Father, through the most holy rosary:

❬ Let us sit at the school of Mary. ℟

❬ Lead us to contemplate with Mary the beauty of the face of Christ. ℟

❬ Grace us to experience the depths of Christ's love. ℟

❬ Help us to go to the very heart of the Christian life. ℟

❬ Enable us to reap the fruits of the liturgy in our daily lives. ℟

❬ Give us a genuine training in holiness. ℟

⬩ Immerse us in contemplation of the mystery of Christ who is our peace. ℟

⬩ Let us be caught up in a clear commitment to advancing peace. ℟

⬩ Provide an effective aid to countering the devastating effects of our age. ℟

⬩ Make us open to receiving the mystery of Trinitarian life. ℟

⬩ Let us share in the memories that Mary recited throughout her life. ℟

⬩ May Mary set before us the mysteries of her Son. ℟

⬩ Give us that remembrance that makes present the works of salvation. ℟

⬩ Open us to the grace that Christ won for us by his life, death, and resurrection. ℟

⬩ Immerse us in the mysteries of the Redeemer's life. ℟

⬩ Enable what Christ has done to shape our existence. ℟

⬩ Give us a way of learning Christ. ℟

⬩ Bless us with a method to discover Christ's secrets and to understand his message. ℟

⬩ May we ask humbly the questions that open us to the light. ℟

⬩ Shape our conduct in accordance with the mind of Christ. ℟

⬩ Conform us to Christ and deepen our friendship with him. ℟

⬩ Let us share Christ's deepest feelings. ℟

⬩ Count us among those Mary continually brings to birth. ℟

⬩ May Mary train us and mold us as she cared for her Son. ℟

⬩ Put us on the path of proclamation and increasing knowledge. ℟

⬩ Lead us through the true doorway to the depths of the heart of Christ. ℟

◦ Bring us to the ocean of joy and light, of suffering and glory. ℟

◦ Awaken in our souls a thirst for a knowledge of Christ continually. ℟

◦ Offer us the secret that leads to a profound, inward knowledge of Christ. ℟

◦ Let us share in the inseparable bond between Christ and his Mother. ℟

◦ Open up the way to the light of the mystery of man. ℟

◦ Permit us to come face to face with the image of the true man. ℟

◦ Help us to hand over our burdens to the merciful hearts of Jesus and Mary. ℟

◦ Mark the rhythm of human life. ℟

◦ Bring human life into harmony with the rhythm of God's own life. ℟

◦ Unite human life in the joyful communion of the Holy Trinity. ℟

◦ Reveal our life's destiny and deepest longing. ℟

◦ Shower me with an outpouring of divine love. ℟

◦ Empower me to enter into the psychological dynamic proper to love. ℟

◦ Help us to be conformed closely to Christ until we attain true holiness. ℟

◦ Communicate yourself to us respecting our human nature. ℟

◦ May we allow you to speak in our hearts. ℟

◦ Give us a share of your own wonder and pleasure before the Blessed Virgin Mary. ℟

◦ Let us set out on the path of assimilation to enter deeply into the life of Christ. ℟

‹ Take us on an inner journey that brings us to living contact with Christ and Mary. ℟

‹ Give us reason to hope for a brighter future. ℟

‹ Let us learn the secret of peace. ℟

‹ Move us to spread around us the true peace of the risen Lord. ℟

‹ Let us encounter Christ in others, especially the most afflicted. ℟

‹ Give us responsible and generous eyes to see the world's problems. ℟

‹ Obtain for us the strength to face difficulties with the certainty of God's help. ℟

‹ Imbue us with the courage to forgive one another. ℟

‹ Let us reproduce in our families the atmosphere of the household of Nazareth. ℟

‹ Give us the way to place our needs and plans in Christ's hands. ℟

‹ Let us draw from Jesus the hope and the strength to go on. ℟

Blessing for the
Vigil of All Saints Day
(October 31)

*In the month of November we celebrate
the Solemnity of All Saints (November 1).
One suggestion is for the family to pray this blessing together
keeping vigil the night before All Saints Day.*

Word of God Col 1: 9-12

WE DO NOT CEASE praying for you and asking that you may be filled with the knowledge of God's will through all spiritual wisdom and understanding to live in a manner worthy of the Lord, so as to be fully pleasing, in every good work bearing fruit and growing in the knowledge of God, strengthened with every power, in accord with his glorious might, for all endurance and patience, with joy giving thanks to the Father, who has made you fit to share in the inheritance of the holy ones in light.

LITANY OF THE COUNSEL OF THE SAINTS

This litany is a meditation on what some of the saints have spoken or written. As we listen to these saints, we pray for a deeper personal participation in their sanctity. This litany represents only a small sampling of the vast communion of saints (the selection is limited due to space constraints). Feel free to add your favorites to it. One option is to sing the litany and its response.

℟ **(Saint's name), pray for us.**

◦ **Holy Mary, Mother of God:** "Behold, I am the handmaid of the Lord. May it be done to me according to your word." ℟

◦ **Saint Gabriel the Archangel:** "Hail, favored one! The Lord is with you." ℟

‣ **Saint Joseph:** [pause in reverent silence] ℟

‣ **Saint John the Baptist:** "Jesus must increase; I must decrease." ℟

‣ **Saint Peter:** "Lord, you know that I love you." ℟

‣ **Saint Paul:** "We had accepted within ourselves the sentence of death, that we might trust not in ourselves but in God who raises the dead." ℟

‣ **Saint Mary Magdalene:** "I have seen the Lord!" ℟

‣ **Saint Ignatius of Antioch:** "There is water living and speaking in me, saying from within me, 'Come to the Father.'" ℟

‣ **Saint Justin Martyr:** "The greatest grace God can give someone is to send him a trial he cannot bear with his own powers – and then sustain him with his grace so he may endure to the end and be saved." ℟

‣ **Saint Irenaeus of Lyons:** "The glory of God is man fully alive." ℟

‣ **Saint Agatha:** "Lord Jesus Christ, you created me, you have watched over me from infancy, kept my body from defilement, preserved me from love of the world, made me able to withstand torture, and granted me the virtue of patience in the midst of torments." ℟

‣ **Saint Cyprian:** "Our union with Christ unifies affections and wills." ℟

‣ **Saint Athanasius:** "It is the Father's glory that man, made and then lost, should be found again; and, when done to death, that he should be made alive, and should become God's temple." ℟

‣ **Saint Ephrem the Syrian:** "O Jesus, in that hour when darkness like a cloak shall be spread over all things, may your grace shine on us in place of the earthly sun." ℟

‣ **Saint Cecilia:** "To die for Christ is not to sacrifice one's youth, but to renew it. Jesus Christ returns a hundredfold for all offered him, and adds to it eternal life." ℟

‹ Saint Basil: "Through the Holy Spirit paradise is restored. We can address God as our Father with confidence; we can share in the grace of Christ." ℟

‹ Saint Gregory Nazianzen: "Each of us can say to the tempter, 'Unlike you, I have not yet become an outcast from heaven through my pride. By my baptism I have become one with him. It is you that should fall prostrate before me.'" ℟

‹ Saint Gregory of Nyssa: "Ideas create idols; only wonder leads to knowing." ℟

‹ Saint Ambrose: "Every soul who has believed both conceives and generates the Word of God and recognizes his works. Let the soul of Mary be in each one of you to magnify the Lord." ℟

‹ Saint John Chrysostom: "Jesus Christ gave you all; he left nothing for himself." ℟

‹ Saint Augustine: "We have been promised something we do not yet possess. It is good for us to persevere in longing until we receive what was promised, and yearning is over." ℟

‹ Saint Peter Chrysologus: "Peace is the plenitude that fulfills our desires. As Christ left the world, he wished to leave the gift he wanted to find when he returned." ℟

‹ Saint Leo the Great: "Let us be raised to the one who made the dust of our lowliness into the body of his glory." ℟

‹ Saint Patrick: "I arise today through the strength of Christ with his baptism, through the strength of his crucifixion with his burial, through the strength of his Resurrection with his Ascension." ℟

‹ Saint Benedict: "What is more delightful than this voice of the Lord calling to us? See how the Lord in his love shows us the way of life." ℟

‹ Saint Columba: "Loving Savior, inspire in us the depth of love that is fitting for you to receive as God." ℟

‹ **Saint Gregory the Great:** "We have been truly set free from subjection to sin because we are united to him who is truly free." ℟

‹ **Saint Maximus the Confessor:** "God made us so that we might become partakers of the divine nature and sharers in his eternity, and so that we might come to be like him through deification by grace." ℟

‹ **Saint Bede the Venerable:** "We should rejoice that the Lord deigns to visit our hearts, and that he deigns to illumine this Passover of our good actions by his benevolent presence." ℟

‹ **Saint Anselm:** "God who made all things made himself of Mary, and thus he refashioned everything he had made." ℟

‹ **Saint Bernard:** "In the measure that grace's kingdom is extended, sin's power is weakened." ℟

‹ **Saint Dominic:** "I shall be more useful to you after my death and I shall help you more effectively than during my life." ℟

‹ **Saint Francis of Assisi:** "May I feel in my heart, as far as possible, that abundance of love with which you, Son of God, were inflamed." ℟

‹ **Saint Anthony of Padua:** "Let us pray that the Lord Jesus Christ pour his grace into us by means of which we ask for and receive the fullness of true joy." ℟

‹ **Saint Clare:** "Live and hope in the Lord, and let your service be according to reason." ℟

‹ **Saint Thomas Aquinas:** "The life of man consists in the love that principally sustains him and in which he finds his greatest satisfaction." ℟

‹ **Saint Gertrude the Great:** "Once again I give you thanks for your merciful love, kindest Lord, for having found another way of arousing me from my inertia." ℟

‹ **Saint Bonaventure:** "God created all things not to increase his glory, but to show it forth and to communicate it." ℟

‹ Saint Catherine of Siena: "When we love something we don't care what sort of abuse or injury or pain we might have to endure to get it; we are concerned only with satisfying our desire for the thing we love." ℟

‹ Saint Joan of Arc: "About Jesus Christ and the Church, I simply know they're just one thing, and we shouldn't complicate the matter." ℟

‹ Saint Bernardine of Siena: "If we but recollect the name of Jesus, it is to fight with confidence – for this name subjects all the fury of our enemies to us." ℟

‹ Saint Catherine of Genoa: "God lets the soul share his goodness so that it becomes one with him. The nearer the soul comes to him, the more it partakes of what is his." ℟

‹ Saint Thomas More: "The brothers of the patriarch Joseph could never have done him so much good with their love and favor as they did him with their malice and hatred." ℟

‹ Saint Angela Merici: "Strengthen, O Lord, my senses and my affections that they may not stray into any betrayal of trust." ℟

‹ Saint Francis Xavier: "God our Lord knows the intentions which he in his mercy has wished to place in us, and the great hope and confidence which he in his goodness has wished that we should have in him." ℟

‹ Saint Ignatius of Loyola: "As long as obedience is flourishing, all the other virtues will be seen to flourish and to bear fruit." ℟

‹ Saint Teresa of Ávila: "Be joyful for there is someone who loves your God as he deserves, who knows him as her only Son." ℟

‹ Saint Charles Borromeo: "The candle that gives light to others must itself be consumed. Thus we also have to act. We ourselves are consumed to give a good example to others." ℟

‹ **Saint Catherine de' Ricci:** "You have been reborn with him through a holy desire to live a new life, looking at yourselves as reflected in his life." ℟

‹ **Saint John of the Cross:** "You considered/ That one hair fluttering at my neck;/ You gazed at it upon my neck/ And it captivated You." ℟

‹ **Saint Aloysius Gonzaga:** "As God is above all created things, honors, possessions, so should our internal esteem of his Divine Majesty surpass our esteem or idea of anything whatever." ℟

‹ **Saint Philip Neri:** "My Jesus, if you want me, cut the fetters that keep me from you." ℟

‹ **Saint Robert Southwell:** "Jesus, possess my mind with your presence and ravish it with your love, that my delight may be to be embraced in the arms of your protection." ℟

‹ **Saint Maria Maddalena de' Pazzi:** "Who doesn't know what God is should apply to Mary. Who doesn't find mercy in God should apply to Mary. Who doesn't have conformity of will should apply to Mary." ℟

‹ **Saint Francis de Sales:** "We must fight our battle between fear and hope in the knowledge that hope is always the stronger because he who comes to our help is almighty." ℟

‹ **Saint Jane Frances de Chantal:** "Oh, how happy is the soul that freely lets herself be molded to the likeness of this divine Savior!" ℟

‹ **Saint Isaac Jogues:** "My hope is in God, who needs not us to accomplish his designs. We must endeavor to be faithful to him." ℟

‹ **Saint Peter Claver:** "Man's salvation and perfection consists in doing the will of God, which he must have in view in all things, and at every moment of his life." ℟

‹ **Saint Vincent de Paul:** "But for divine grace I would be in temper hard and repellant, rough and crabbed." ℟

‹ Saint John Eudes: "With his own hand God the Father has impressed on Mary's heart a perfect semblance of the divine qualities of his love." ℟

‹ Saint Claude de la Colombière: "My Jesus, let me live in your heart and pour all my bitterness into it where it will be utterly consumed." ℟

‹ Saint Margaret Mary Alacoque: "All my pleasure in this land of exile is that of having every kind of suffering found on the cross, deprived of every other consolation except that of the Sacred Heart." ℟

‹ Saint Louis Grignion de Montfort: "In Mary alone, by the grace of Jesus Christ, man is made godlike as far as human nature is capable of it." ℟

‹ Saint Paul of the Cross: "The soul whom God wants to draw to deepest union with him by means of holy prayer must pass through the way of suffering during prayer." ℟

‹ Saint Alphonsus Liguori: "We must love God in the way that pleases him, and not just in a way that suits ourselves. God wishes people to empty themselves of everything and to be filled with his divine love." ℟

‹ Saint Elizabeth Ann Seton: "O Jesus, sure joy of my soul, give me but a true love of you. Let me seek you as my only good." ℟

‹ Saint John Vianney: "The soul can feed only on God; only God can suffice it; only God can fill it; only God can satiate its hunger. Its God is absolutely necessary to it." ℟

‹ Saint John Neumann: "Though God hates sin more than any other thing, he loves us poor miserable sinners. He ardently desires the welfare of our souls as if his own happiness depended on it." ℟

‹ Saint Peter Julian Eymard: "Abide in the home of the divine and fatherly goodness of God like his child who knows nothing, does nothing, makes a mess of everything, but nevertheless lives in his goodness." ℟

◁ **Saint John Bosco:** "What tenderness there is in Jesus' love for man! In his infinite goodness, he established, with each of us, bonds of sublime love! His love has no limits." ℟

◁ **Saint Thérèse of Lisieux:** "You alone, O Jesus, could satisfy a soul that needed to love even to the infinite." ℟

◁ **Saint Bernadette Soubirous:** "O Mary, Mother of Sorrows, I am the child of your sorrows. My tender Mother, here is your child, who can do no more. Have pity on me." ℟

◁ **Saint Frances Xavier Cabrini:** "Stretch every fiber of my being, dear Lord, that I may more easily fly toward you. May your Spirit which once breathed over the chaos of the earth give life to all the powers of my soul." ℟

◁ **Saint Maximilian Kolbe:** "Shall the urge for complete and total happiness, inherent to human nature, be the only need to remain unfulfilled and unsatisfied? No, even this longing can be fulfilled by the infinite and eternal God." ℟

◁ **Saint Teresa Benedicta of the Cross:** "Holy realism has a certain affinity with the realism of the child who receives and responds to impressions with unimpaired vigor and vitality, and with uninhibited simplicity." ℟

◁ **Saint Katharine Drexel:** "May your faith be increased so as to realize the fact that you are never alone, wheresoever you may be, that the great God is with you, in you." ℟

◁ **Saint Faustina:** "Jesus, I trust in you." ℟

◁ **Saint Pius of Pietrelcina:** "If the soul longs for nothing else than to love its God then don't worry and be quite sure that this soul possesses everything, that it possesses God himself." ℟

◁ **Saint Damien Joseph de Veuster of Moloka'i:** "In the face of the too real dangers that surround me I repeat: 'Lord, I have placed all my hope in you. I will never be confounded.'" ℟

A Thanksgiving Day Grace

OPENING PRAYER

LEADER 1:

Let us pray. Most merciful Father, your gifts of love are countless and your goodness infinite. On this Thanksgiving Day we come before you with gratitude for your kindness: open our hearts to concern for others so that we may share your gifts of loving service with all your people. We ask this through our Lord Jesus Christ, your Son, who lives and reigns with you and the Holy Spirit, one God, for ever and ever.

All: Amen.

WORD OF GOD

LEADER 2:

Luke 17: 12-19

As [JESUS] was entering a village, ten lepers met [him]. They stood at a distance from him and raised their voice, saying, "Jesus, Master! Have pity on us!" And when he saw them, he said, "Go show your-selves to the priests." As they were going they were cleansed. And one of them, realizing he had been healed, returned, glorifying God in a loud voice; and he fell at the feet of Jesus and thanked him. He was a Samaritan. Jesus said in reply, "Ten were cleansed, were they not? Where are the other nine? Has none but this for-eigner returned to give thanks to God?" Then he said to him, "Stand up and go; your faith has saved you."

RESPONSORIAL PSALM

℟ **For his love endures for ever.**

LEADER 3:

> Praise the Lord, who is so good. ℟
> Praise the God of gods. ℟
> Praise the Lord of lords. ℟
>
> [He] freed us from our foes. ℟
> And gives food to all flesh. ℟
> Praise the God of heaven. ℟

> (Ps 136: 1-3, 24-26)

LITANY OF THANKSGIVING

℟ **We thank you, O Lord.**

LEADER 1:

‹ This is a day to thank God for all his many blessings in our lives. With gratitude we now say: For the love of God, for faith, family, and friends: ℟

LEADER 2:

‹ For joys, successes, achievements, and accomplishments: ℟

LEADER 3:

‹ For health, safety, work, and rest: ℟

LEADER 1:

‹ For struggles, sorrows, trials, and sufferings: ℟

LEADER 2:

◄ For our jobs, for those who support us, for our education, and for the chance to serve: ℞

LEADER 3:

◄ For our gifts, talents, and abilities, for honors, for strength and energy: ℞

LEADER 1:

◄ For our homes, for food, warmth, and shelter, for all the things that have made us happy: ℞

LEADER 2:

◄ For our hobbies and pets, for happy memories, for our favorite things, for leisure and relaxation: ℞

LEADER 3:

◄ For our nation, for freedom and peace, for teachers, leaders, and those who give us good example: ℞

LEADER 1:

◄ For the ability to say "I'm sorry," for the grace of repentance, for the forgiveness of others, for the generosity of others: ℞

LEADER 2:

◄ For good advice, for financial security, for the trust others put in us, for tenderness, understanding, and compassion: ℞

LEADER 3:

◄ For kindness, goodness, joy, and laughter, for the times we have helped others or made them happy: ℞

LEADER 1:

⟨ For all the wonders of creation, for beauty, music, sports, and art, for new opportunities and second chances: ℟

LEADER 2:

⟨ For failures and rejection, for all the ways we have grown up and become better people: ℟

LEADER 3:

⟨ For renewed hope and fulfilled dreams, for the providence and protection of heaven: ℟

LEADER 1:

⟨ For the gift of life: ℟

Closing Prayer

LORD JESUS, we give you thanks, not only with the lips and heart, which often comes to little, but with the spirit, with which we speak to you, question you, love you, and recognize you. You are our all, and everything is in you. In you we live, and move, and have our being. You are our father, our brother, our all; and to those who love you, you have promised such things as no one has ever seen or thought of, no one ever enjoyed. Make the gift of these things to your humble faithful; you who are God, true and good, and there is no other besides you. You are the true God, the true Son of God, to whom be honor and glory and majesty in eternity and for all ages to come.

Gallican Formularies

Blessings for Spiritual Growth

Blessing to
Live Deeply

WORD OF GOD

SUNDAY

Here deep calls to deep in the roar of your torrents./ All your waves and breakers sweep over me./ At dawn may the LORD bestow faithful love/ that I may sing praise through the night,/ praise to the God of my life. (Ps 42: 8-9)

MONDAY

After [Jesus] had finished speaking, he said to Simon, "Put out into deep water and lower your nets for a catch." (Lk 5: 4)

TUESDAY

I urge you therefore, brothers, by the mercies of God, to offer your bodies as a living sacrifice, holy and pleasing to God, your spiritual worship. Do not conform yourselves to this age but be transformed by the renewal of your mind, that you may discern what is the will of God, what is good and pleasing and perfect. (Rom 12: 1-2)

WEDNESDAY

"For where your treasure is, there also will your heart be." (Mt 6: 21)

THURSDAY

"Some [seed] fell on rocky ground, where it had little soil. It sprang up at once because the soil was not deep." (Mt 13: 5)

FRIDAY

"From within people, from their hearts, come evil thoughts, unchastity, theft, murder, adultery, greed, malice, deceit, licentiousness, envy, blasphemy, arrogance, folly. All these evils come from within and they defile." (Mk 7: 21-23)

SATURDAY

As it is written:/ "What eye has not seen, and ear has not heard,/ and what has not entered the human heart,/ what God has prepared for those who love him,"/ this God has revealed to us through the Spirit.
For the Spirit scrutinizes everything, even the depths of God. (1 Cor 2: 9-10)

LITANY FOR
"PUTTING OUT INTO THE DEEP"

℟ **Lord, deliver me.**

‹ From whatever is frivolous or shallow: ℟

‹ From self-absorption: ℟

‹ From impatience and paltriness: ℟

‹ From all fretfulness and fussiness: ℟

‹ From selfishness and disregard: ℟

‹ From insecurity and fear: ℟

‹ From fascination with lesser things: ℟

‹ From ambition: ℟

‹ From individualism: ℟

‹ From lack of prayer: ℟

‹ From trifling matters: ℟

‹ From negativity: ℟

‹ From all pettiness and petulance: ℟

‹ From disordered priorities: ℟

‹ From living according to the flesh: ℟

‹ From judging by appearances: ℟

‹ From cynicism: ℟

‹ From activism: ℟

‹ From all that is vapid and venal: ℟

‹ From the pressure to conform to things beneath me: ℟

‹ From vanity: ℟

‹ From propaganda and worldly notions: ℟

‹ From whatever is trivial or superficial: ℟

‹ From living only for pleasure: ℟

‹ From daydreaming: ℟

‹ From rumor and gossip: ℟

‹ From whatever is carnal or coarse: ℟

‹ From the grip of grudges and resentment: ℟

‹ From the temptation to make mountains out of molehills: ℟

‹ From preconceptions, presumption, and prejudice: ℟

‹ From fantasies and passing fancies: ℟

‹ From worry over things that don't really matter: ℟

‹ From distractions: ℟

‹ From weakness and cowardice: ℟

‹ **From procrastination:** ℞

‹ **From unnecessary agitation and conflict:** ℞

‹ **From the refusal to make commitments:** ℞

‹ **From whatever is banal or debasing:** ℞

‹ **From hairsplitting and nitpicking:** ℞

‹ **From complaining:** ℞

‹ **From self-indulgence:** ℞

‹ **From materialism:** ℞

‹ **From useless anxiety:** ℞

‹ **From micromanaging:** ℞

‹ **From willfulness:** ℞

‹ **From meaningless preoccupations:** ℞

‹ **From living on the surface:** ℞

‹ **From disordered self-assertion:** ℞

‹ **From dissent to the truth:** ℞

Closing Prayer

MOST MERCIFUL FATHER, I want to live more deeply in the Truth. Help me to live more deeply in the Truth. In the words of your servant, Blessed Elizabeth of the Trinity, "may each minute bring me more deeply into your mystery." Fill my heart with your love and your grace so that my life may become a profound reflection of your greatness and glory. Through Christ our Lord.

Blessing to
Aid Our Efforts at Prayer

"Prayer… is always contact with God and means leaving disper-siveness behind us and entering into recollection – not in order to be alone, but in order to be close to him."

Blessed John Paul II

Blessed John Paul II has written that prayer "is always God's initia-tive within us. This initiative restores in us our true humanity; it restores in us our unique dignity." The following litany is meant to help believers enter into this divine initiative while at the same time leaving behind all distractions.

℟ **Lord Jesus Christ, Son of the living God, have mercy on me, a sinner.**

◖ Without prayer I forget that for me to be is to depend, so I beg, ℟

◖ Even though I feel unworthy of a relationship with you, ℟

◖ Distractions and temptations torment me from every side, but, ℟

◖ When I don't know the words or the right way to pray, ℟

◖ It's so hard to be silent, centered, and still, so, ℟

◖ Prayer is the way that I educate my heart, so, ℟

◖ My defects and failings discourage me from praying; please, ℟

◖ It's easy to doubt the good prayer can do and to see it as a waste of time, so I beg, ℟

◖ When I'm embarrassed to pray, or tempted to see it as a sign of weakness, ℟

‹ Save me from comparing myself to others, from trying to impress you with my virtues. ℟

‹ I feel so arid, so listless and empty, but, ℟

‹ When I resist prayer because fatalism tells me that I can never change, ℟

‹ Since prayer is the only gesture that totally realizes the human being's stature, ℟

‹ My attempts at prayer are crippled because I am so critical of others; please, ℟

‹ When self-righteousness seduces me to think that I am "beyond" prayer, ℟

‹ We are made as attraction and thirst for life, so I ask in prayer, ℟

‹ Without prayer you become an abstraction, and so I cry, ℟

‹ It's so easy to get cynical, skeptical, and snide. ℟

‹ All you ask for in prayer is a heart given over to you. ℟

‹ The height of prayer is seeing the depths as if they were everyday things. ℟

‹ Let me always remember that prayer is your gift. ℟

‹ Prayer is the recognition of the Presence that is my destiny. ℟

Blessing of the
Holy Name of Jesus

One mark of the greatness of human dignity is that God lets Adam name the newly created animals (Gn 2: 19-20). This divine favor reaches its zenith when the Father commands the Virgin Mary and Saint Joseph to name his incarnate Son: "You shall name him Jesus" (see Lk 1: 31 and Mt 1: 21). We are blessed to share in this incomparable privilege of "naming Jesus." And we do so frequently, with fervor and conviction, for, as Saint Peter professes, "There is no… other name under heaven given to the human race by which we are to be saved" (Acts 4: 12).

By praying the Holy Name of Jesus, we honor the wish Christ made the night before he died: "Whatever you ask in my name, I will do" (Jn 14: 13; see also v. 14). The Lord uses the occasion of a Resurrection appearance to his disciples to remind all believers of the power that is theirs through the invocation of the Holy Name of Jesus: "In my name they will drive out demons, they will speak new languages… They will lay hands on the sick, and they will recover" (Mk 16: 17-18). For "the name of Jesus is the highest honor of the believer" (Saint Bernardine of Siena).

LITANY OF THE GRACES OF
THE HOLY NAME OF JESUS

℟ **Lord Jesus, save us.**

LORD JESUS,

‹ **Your Holy Name fully manifests the supreme power of the Name that is above every name.** ℟

‹ **Your Holy Name is the name that contains everything.** ℟

‹ **Your Holy Name is at the heart of all Christian prayer.** ℟

‹ To say that Holy Name of Jesus in prayer is to call you within ourselves. ℟

‹ When we repeat your Holy Name with a humble and attentive heart, our prayer brings forth fruit with patience. ℟

‹ We are able to pray always through the supreme gift of your Holy Name. ℟

‹ By the power of your Holy Name, we are washed, we are sanctified, and we are justified. ℟

‹ Our continual confession of your Holy Name brings us remission of sins, healing, and enlightenment. ℟

‹ Your Holy Name lifts us up from loneliness, from isolation, from discouragement, from fear. ℟

‹ By giving us your Holy Name you reveal to us your faithfulness. ℟

‹ To utter your Holy Name is to be blessed with the assurance of your presence – that you are with us always, even until the end of time. ℟

‹ Your Holy Name gives us solace in suffering. ℟

‹ Blessed with your Holy Name, we know that we are not alone in the problems that afflict us. ℟

‹ The grace of your Holy Name enables us to leave behind our false self. ℟

‹ Through the invocation of your Holy Name I experience anew your forgiveness of my sins. ℟

‹ The gift of your Holy Name frees us from doubt, enlightens our darkness, and brings assurance and hope in the face of the world's emptiness. ℟

‹ When I am without adequate words to adore you, I can always say: ℟

‹ Your Holy Name brings us strength when we are tempted. ℟

‹ Through the gift of your Holy Name we are ever certain that you have come close to us. ℟

‹ Through the utterance of your Holy Name we are transformed and made a new creation. ℟

‹ Your Holy Name beckons us to the deepest experience of union. ℟

‹ You have called us not servants but friends, and we know that that friendship is real whenever we say your Holy Name. ℟

A Pauline Blessing for
Continued Conversion

"Conversion to God always consists in discovering his mercy."

Blessed John Paul II

REFLECTION ON CONVERSION

"Before his conversion, Paul had not been a man distant from God… In the light of the encounter with Christ, however, he understood that with this he had sought to build up himself and his own justice, and that with all this justice he had lived for himself. He realized that a new approach in his life was absolutely essential. And we find this new approach expressed in his words: 'The life I now live in the flesh I live by faith in the Son of God, who loved me and gave himself for me' (Gal 2: 20). Paul, therefore, no longer lives for himself, for his own justice. He lives for Christ and with Christ: in giving of himself, he is no longer seeking and building himself up. This is the new justice, the new orientation given to us by the Lord, given to us by faith… From here we draw a very important lesson: what counts is to place Jesus Christ at the center of our lives, so that our identity is marked essentially by the encounter, by communion with Christ and with his Word."

Pope Benedict XVI

WORD OF GOD

SUNDAY

Whoever is in Christ is a new creation: the old things have passed away; behold, new things have come. And all this is from God, who has reconciled us to himself through Christ. (2 Cor 5: 17-18)

MONDAY

Our salvation is nearer now than when we first believed; the night is advanced, the day is at hand. Let us then throw off the works of darkness [and] put on the armor of light. (Rom 13: 11b-12)

TUESDAY

Working together, then, we appeal to you not to receive the grace of God in vain. For he says:/ "In an acceptable time I heard you,/ and on the day of salvation I helped you."/ Behold, now is a very acceptable time; behold, now is the day of salvation. (2 Cor 6: 1-2)

WEDNESDAY

Do you not know that the runners in the stadium all run in the race, but only one wins the prize? Run so as to win. (1 Cor 9: 24)

THURSDAY

We are not discouraged; rather, although our outer self is wasting away, our inner self is being renewed day by day. (2 Cor 4: 16)

FRIDAY

A thorn in the flesh was given to me, an angel of Satan, to beat me, to keep me from being too elated. Three times I begged the Lord about this, that it might leave me, but he said to me, "My grace is sufficient for you, for power is made perfect in weakness." (2 Cor 12: 7-9a)

SATURDAY

But since we are of the day, let us be sober, putting on the breastplate of faith and love and the helmet that is hope for salvation. For God did not destine us for wrath, but to gain salvation through our Lord Jesus Christ. (1 Thes 5: 8-9)

LITANY OF ONGOING CONVERSION

*"Only those who continue in their conversion truly know God"
(Abbot André Louf). What does this mean concretely for us?
"Conversion involves the transformation of all our fragmented
experiences, all our disjointed and painful memories, all our
divisive and frustrating moments of unachieved hopes, yearn-
ings, and dreams, as well as our failures and loss of self-esteem
or sense of worth resulting from the destructive power of evil"
(M. Gaudoin-Parker). United in the mystery of the conversion of
Saint Paul, we pray for the graces of conversion in our own life.*

℟ **Lord, give me the grace of conversion.**

LORD JESUS,

‣ When I look at my life from the starting point of my own
insufficiencies instead of from the fact of your compassion, grace,
and love for me: ℟

‣ When I would prefer to live by my own thoughts and my own
understanding instead of by your Truth which alone can set me
free: ℟

‣ When I would rather brood over what annoys me than turn
myself over to you who always invite me to come to you: ℟

‣ When I obsess over self-absorption, complacency, and
self-assertiveness: ℟

‣ When I get dejected about my sin, not because it offends you,
but because it prevents me from being able to take delight in
myself: ℟

‣ Whenever I live in a dualistic way, as if my faith and my "real
life" are two separate things: ℟

‣ When I am deceived into thinking that my happiness depends
on something in the future instead of what you give me in the
present moment: ℟

‹ When discouragement and shame make it hard for me to be faithful: ℟

‹ When I become distraught over the evil I would commit if left to myself, forgetting that I do not live according to myself but that I live in you: ℟

‹ When self-doubt and fear seem to have the last say: ℟

‹ When I miss the point of my fragility, a gift you give me so that I will always be prompted to rely on you: ℟

‹ When I am inclined to interpret my problems as punishment and my miseries as being abandoned by God: ℟

‹ When impenetrability takes over my life, making me resistant to your beauty and all the little ways you ordain to give yourself to me: ℟

‹ When I get distracted by my feelings, my emotions, my passions, my regrets: ℟

‹ When I get duped into thinking that I must fix myself up in order to have a relationship with you, forgetting that you come to me with your love just the way I am: ℟

‹ When I treat my faith like some abstract answer to be sought instead of as a loving Presence to be affirmed: ℟

‹ When I get discouraged by chronic or recurring sins in my life: ℟

‹ When I would attempt to earn your favor by my achievements, forgetting that I did not choose you, but it is you who chose me: ℟

‹ When scandalized by my own selfishness and self-assertion: ℟

‹ When the meaninglessness in my life makes me ignore or reduce the desires of my heart that lead me to you: ℟

‹ When independence and self-sufficiency make me resist the companionship with others through which you will to give me your friendship and tenderness: ℟

‹ Whenever I treat my preconceptions like idols that drain my life of wonder and simplicity: ℟

‹ When the evidence of all that is wrong with my life leads me to become paralyzed, indifferent, or lax: ℟

‹ When I get preoccupied with all my self-justifications trying to convince myself that I am lovable: ℟

‹ When I would rather live my life in a safe or sheltered way instead of living my life as a risk, putting your will first in all things: ℟

‹ When the daily inner rebellion makes me cynical and negative about what really matters most: ℟

‹ When my misgivings keep me from receiving the fresh embrace of love you offer me at every moment: ℟

CLOSING PRAYER
(Based on the writings of Pope Benedict XVI)

LOVING FATHER, Christian conversion calls for going beyond self-reliance and for entrusting ourselves to the Mystery. Those who want to find you need, again and again, an inner conversion, a new direction. Conversion is first and foremost your gift that opens a heart to your infinite goodness. Give me the grace to turn around inside, to be won over by Jesus, and so to live always for you. We ask this united with the intercession of the great Apostle Paul through Christ our Lord.

Blessing for the
Growth of Freedom

We place before the Lord whatever constricts our capacity for God so that we might share in the graces proclaimed in the Exsultet: *Christ has "ransomed us with his blood" and "freed the people of Israel from their slavery." The Easter Vigil is the night that "Christians everywhere are freed from all defilement" and that "Jesus Christ broke the chains of death." For "to ransom a slave" the Father "gave away" his Son.*

MEDITATION

"Freedom is a complete purity and detachment which seeks the Eternal. A free soul dismisses all defect, and penetrates into the uncreated good, that is God, and acquires it. A free soul does not let itself be drawn away by anything that might separate it or mediate between it and God. A free soul seizes and wins all virtue, and not only virtue, but also the essence of virtue. And then is the soul thoroughly free, when she can only endure what is best and entirely abandons evil. Genuine freedom is so noble that no one gives it save God the Father."

Father John Tauler, O.P.

WORD OF GOD

SUNDAY

"If you remain in my word, you will truly be my disciples, and you will know the truth, and the truth will set you free." (Jn 8: 31-32)

MONDAY

For creation was made subject to futility, not of its own accord but because of the one who subjected it, in hope that creation itself would be set free from slavery to corruption and share in the glorious freedom of the children of God. (Rom 8: 20-21)

TUESDAY

Now the Lord is the Spirit, and where the Spirit of the Lord is, there is freedom. (2 Cor 3: 17)

WEDNESDAY

For you were called for freedom, brothers. But do not use this freedom as an opportunity for the flesh; rather, serve one another through love. (Gal 5: 13)

THURSDAY

The one who peers into the perfect law of freedom and perseveres, and is not a hearer who forgets but a doer who acts, such a one shall be blessed in what he does.
So speak and so act as people who will be judged by the law of freedom. (Jas 1: 25; 2: 12)

FRIDAY

Now since the children share in blood and flesh, [Jesus] likewise shared in them, that through death he might destroy the one who has the power of death, that is, the devil, and free those who through fear of death had been subject to slavery all their life. (Heb 2: 14-15)

SATURDAY

Be free, yet without using freedom as a pretext for evil, but as slaves of God. (1 Pt 2: 16)

LITANY OF FREEDOM

"For freedom Christ set us free" (Gal 5: 1). With longing to grow in Gospel freedom, we pray:

℟ **Lord, by your truth, set us free.**

- Where there is hatred and warfare: ℞
- Where there is slavery and oppression: ℞
- Where there is conflict and division: ℞
- Where there is darkness and despair: ℞
- Where there is hostility and aggression: ℞
- Where there is ignorance and doubt: ℞
- Where there is prejudice and discrimination: ℞
- Where there is brutality and ruthlessness: ℞
- Where there is sin and self-exaltation: ℞
- Where there is addiction and destructive behavior: ℞
- Where there is apathy and indifference: ℞
- Where there is temptation and trial: ℞
- Where there is error and dissension: ℞
- Where there is enmity and animosity: ℞
- Where there is vanity and self-sufficiency: ℞
- Where there is malice and meanness: ℞
- Where there is irreligion and disbelief: ℞
- Where there is pettiness and petulance: ℞
- Where there is censure and reproach: ℞
- Where there is pressure and stress: ℞
- Where there is domination and subservience: ℞
- Where there is iniquity and evil: ℞
- Where there is compromise and constriction: ℞
- Where there is denial and delinquency: ℞
- Where there is insecurity and self-doubt: ℞

- Where there is tyranny and treachery: ℟
- Where there is anxiety and worry: ℟
- Where there is vindictiveness and vengefulness: ℟
- Where there is poverty and strife: ℟
- Where there is permissiveness and irresponsibility: ℟
- Where there is anarchy and confusion: ℟
- Where there is malevolence and vice: ℟
- Where there is defeatism and despondency: ℟
- Where there is fear and trepidation: ℟
- Where there is violence and injury: ℟
- Where there is possessiveness and attachment: ℟
- Where there is divisiveness and detraction: ℟
- Where there is obsession and compulsion: ℟
- Where there is insolence and indignation: ℟
- Where there is rancor and spite: ℟
- Where there is deception and delusion: ℟
- Where there is obstinacy and stubbornness: ℟
- Where there is selfishness and avarice: ℟
- Where there is opposition and frustration: ℟
- Where there is indecision and passiveness: ℟
- Where there is resentment and bitterness: ℟
- Where there is controversy and contradiction: ℟
- Where there is infidelity and deceit: ℟
- Where there is callousness and coldness: ℟
- Where there is retribution and retaliation: ℟

- Where there is chaos and disorder: ℞
- Where there is suspicion and second-guessing: ℞
- Where there is envy and jealousy: ℞
- Where there is self-righteousness and self-seeking: ℞
- Where there is pride and egoism: ℞
- Where there is indolence and inertia: ℞
- Where there is ambition and exploitation: ℞
- Where there is derision and scorn: ℞
- Where there is thoughtlessness and neglect: ℞
- Where there is arrogance and manipulation: ℞
- Where there is activism and distraction: ℞
- Where there is false judgment and harsh criticism: ℞
- Where there is coercion and duress: ℞
- Where there is exclusion and marginalization: ℞
- Where there is negativity and skepticism: ℞
- Where there is self-indulgence and diffidence: ℞
- Where there is hopelessness and fatalism: ℞
- Where there is disunity and discord: ℞
- Where there is sarcasm and cynicism: ℞
- Where there is torpor and sloth: ℞
- Where there is lawlessness and fury: ℞
- Where there is insincerity and hypocrisy: ℞
- Where there is materialism and greed: ℞
- Where there is depression and dejection: ℞
- Where there is ingratitude and presumption: ℞

- Where there is trouble and contention: ℟
- Where there is sensuality and anger: ℟
- Where there is disobedience and defiance: ℟
- Where there is disrespect and abuse: ℟
- Where there is disloyalty and inconstancy: ℟
- Where there is superficiality and shallowness: ℟
- Where there is indignity and disgrace: ℟
- Where there is reprisal and condemnation: ℟
- Where there is lukewarmness and laxity: ℟
- Where there is contempt and disdain: ℟
- Where there is disregard and lethargy: ℟
- Where there is impiety and godlessness: ℟

CLOSING PRAYER

LORD JESUS, when you raised Lazarus from the dead, you commanded those attending his tomb: "Unbind him and let him go free!" Freedom is the outstanding manifestation of the divine image in us. Free us from all that inhibits and enslaves us. Renew our capacity for God so that our freedom may be a force for growth and maturity in truth and goodness. We ask this in your holy name.

Blessing of the
Mysteries of Christ's Life

Word of God   Ephesians 1: 8b-10

IN ALL WISDOM and insight, [God] has made known to us the mystery of his will in accord with his favor that he set forth in [Jesus Christ] as a plan for the fullness of times, to sum up all things in Christ, in heaven and on earth.

LITANY OF THE MYSTERIES OF
THE LIFE OF THE LORD

℟ Christ, be our life.

LOVING FATHER,

‣ At the Annunciation your angel offered the human presence of your Son to the Blessed Virgin Mary; let my daily "yes" to this Presence be one with Mary's. ℟

‣ The Birth of Jesus blesses us with the companionship that our hearts so crave; let my life be lived in prayer before the event of God-with-us. ℟

‣ At the Epiphany the Magi gave homage to your Son and, in that acknowledgment, were given a new way to live; let me live by such faith always. ℟

‣ At the Presentation in the Temple, Joseph and Mary offered your Son to you in a gesture of sacrifice; may my life be a sacrificial gift of self. ℟

‣ At the Finding in the Temple, Mary discovered the depth of her Son's passion for you; let me always live with zeal to do your will. ℟

‹ At the Baptism of the Lord, your Son identified himself with sinners; let my sinfulness lead me to greater confidence in your mercy, for you love to be acknowledged by nothingness. ℟

‹ At the Temptations in the Desert, Satan tried to persuade Jesus to renounce his Sonship; let every temptation of my life lead me to greater dependency on my relationship with you. ℟

‹ Through the Preaching of the Kingdom, the world heard a Word that filled them with hope; make me alert and obedient to every utterance of your Son. ℟

‹ The Miracles of Jesus are events that reveal a new humanity and that beckon us to our destiny; through the countless miracles I encounter every day, help me to live in perfect awareness in front of reality. ℟

‹ Through the Transfiguration, your love for your Son became radiant and resplendent; let me live in the gaze of Jesus so that I may be transformed in him. ℟

‹ At the Last Supper, your Son gave us the gift of himself so that we would never be without his real Presence; may this Holy Communion be for me an inner dimension at the source of all my thoughts and actions. ℟

‹ The Passion of your Son is the expression of the most perfect human freedom; may I find meaning in all my suffering by adhering unfailingly to Christ crucified. ℟

‹ The proof of the Resurrection is the fact that your people have always stayed together through the Presence of your risen Son; make that companionship and belonging grow through my missionary love. ℟

‹ The Ascension gives witness to the truth that the purest love is love that neither manipulates nor possesses; through the mystery of the Ascension make my love virginal. ℟

‹ Pentecost attests that the Holy Spirit constantly comes to make Jesus present; come, Holy Spirit – come through Mary. ℟

Blessing for the
Wisdom of the
Doctors of the Church

Blessed John Paul II encouraged us to rely on the doctrine taught by the Church's proclaimed Doctors of the Church because "it sheds new light on the mysteries of the faith – a deeper understanding of Christ's mystery."

This blessing might be broken down into a number of parts that can be shared by different members of the family.

Most merciful Father, you have blessed the Doctors of the Church with an ardent love of the truth. May the divine wisdom that distinguished their graced teaching form my spiritual life so that I may share also in the splendor of their holiness.

℟ Pray for us.

‹ Saint Hilary of Poitiers († 368): "In God's presence, let an understanding which attempts to comprehend admit its own limitation."
– For a heart filled with wonder before God's mystery, Saint Hilary: ℟

‹ Saint Athanasius († 373): "The all-holy Son of the Father came to our realms to renew man who had been made in his likeness."
– For freedom from a wicked conformity to self, Saint Athanasius: ℟

‹ Saint Ephrem the Syrian († 373): "The Lord who is beyond measure measures out nourishment to all, adapting his blessing to our appetite."
– For the purification of my desires, Saint Ephrem: ℟

‹ Saint Basil the Great († 379): "Silence is the beginning of purification in the soul."
– For fidelity in making time for sacred silence each day, Saint Basil: ℟

‹ Saint Cyril of Jerusalem († 386): "Let the truth of God sink into your soul to be its foundation stone."
– For the grace to live more deeply by the truth, Saint Cyril of Jerusalem: ℟

‹ Saint Gregory Nazianzen († 390): "Worship him who was hung on the cross because of you, even if you are hanging there yourself."
– For the perseverance to pray in times of trial and distress, Saint Gregory: ℟

‹ Saint Ambrose († 397): "See how many masters have those who do not want to have the only Lord."
– For steadfastness and singleness of heart, Saint Ambrose: ℟

‹ Saint John Chrysostom († 407): "In showing his wounds, Christ shows the efficacy of the cross, by which he gives all good things, which is peace."
– For the strength to accept suffering in my life, Saint John Chrysostom: ℟

‹ Saint Jerome († 420): "When pride raises up a man, it at the same time abases him, for by his sin it makes him an enemy of God."
– For humility, simplicity, and docility, Saint Jerome: ℟

‹ Saint Augustine († 430): "This is the poison of your error: you claim to make the grace of Christ consist in his example and not in the gift of his Person."
– For the grace to follow Jesus in friendship, Saint Augustine: ℟

‹ Saint Cyril of Alexandria († 444): "Because the Son is God from God, in some mysterious way he passes this honor on to us."
– For a greater share in the sonship of Jesus, Saint Cyril of Alexandria: ℟

‹ Saint Peter Chrysologus († 450): "He who bears mercy and carries love does not know how to grow weary."
– For a compassionate and merciful heart, Saint Peter Chrysologus: ℞

‹ Saint Leo the Great († 461): "There was no other reason for the Son of God to be born than that he might be fixed to a cross."
– For the grace to embrace the cross of Jesus Christ crucified, Saint Leo: ℞

‹ Saint Gregory the Great († 604): "Fittingly did the Spirit appear in fire; in every heart that he enters, he kindles the desire of his own eternity."
– For release from the torpor of spiritual coldness, Saint Gregory the Great: ℞

‹ Saint Isidore of Seville († c. 636): "All hope consists in confession. Do not doubt, do not hesitate, never despair of the mercy of God."
– For renewed repentance and frequent confession, Saint Isidore: ℞

‹ Saint Bede the Venerable († 735): "To ask God for the justice of his kingdom is to ask principally for faith, hope, and love."
– For the end of all false justification in my life, Saint Bede: ℞

‹ Saint John Damascene († 749): "We fasten souls to the Blessed Virgin Mary, our hope, as to a firm anchor."
– For unwavering confidence in Mary's maternal mediation, Saint John Damascene: ℞

‹ Saint Peter Damian († 1072): "The mystery of holy Church's inward unity can never be marred in its integrity."
– For the renewal of the Church in holiness, Saint Peter Damian: ℞

‹ Saint Anselm († 1109): "Your sole concern should be the establishment of God's reign in your heart, and the life of your soul should be the life of God himself."
– For the grace to live for God, Saint Anselm: ℞

‹ Saint Bernard of Clairvaux († 1153): "God did not wish us to have anything which had not passed through Mary's hands."
– For greater devotion to the Blessed Virgin Mary, Saint Bernard: ℟

‹ Saint Anthony of Padua († 1231): "Happy the man whose words issue from the Holy Spirit and not from himself."
– For holiness in all my conversations, Saint Anthony of Padua: ℟

‹ Saint Bonaventure († 1274): "When the flesh is subjected to the spirit, inner peace and joy are restored to the soul."
– For total abandonment to the life of the Spirit, Saint Bonaventure: ℟

‹ Saint Thomas Aquinas († 1274): "Christ would not be so intimately united to us were we to share only in his power; how much better that he should give us his very self."
– For a deeper love of the Holy Eucharist, Saint Thomas Aquinas: ℟

‹ Saint Albert the Great († 1280): "In all simplicity and confidence abandon yourself without reserve to God's unfailing providence."
– For perfect surrender to the will of God, Saint Albert: ℟

‹ Saint Catherine of Siena († 1380): "Make a sweet dwelling in the side of Christ crucified in order to have a holy knowledge of yourself."
– For the grace of self-knowledge, Saint Catherine: ℟

‹ Saint John of Ávila († 1569): "Even our evil does not impede the surpassing goodness by which God desires to save the good that he created and to destroy the evil that we committed."
– For hope in God's unfailing goodness, Saint John of Ávila: ℟

‹ Saint Teresa of Ávila († 1582): "The Lord does not care so much for the importance of our works as for the love with which they are done."
– For absolute purity of intention and unfailing love, Saint Teresa of Ávila: ℟

‹ **Saint John of the Cross** († 1591): "When once the will is touched by God himself, it cannot be satisfied except by God."
– For a conversion that orders all my longings, Saint John of the Cross: ℟

‹ **Saint Peter Canisius** († 1597): "Let the world indulge its madness. But we, buried deep in the wounds of Christ, why should we be dismayed?"
– For resoluteness, constant trust, and hope, Saint Peter Canisius: ℟

‹ **Saint Lawrence of Brindisi** († 1619): "Against the world, the flesh, and the devil, the Word of God serves as a sword that destroys all sin."
– For a deeper love of God's holy Word, Saint Lawrence: ℟

‹ **Saint Robert Bellarmine** († 1621): "Nothing serves so well to maintain peace and union as the charity by which we put up with another's defects."
– For patience, tolerance, compassion, and a forgiving spirit, Saint Robert: ℟

‹ **Saint Francis de Sales** († 1622): "On the tree of the cross, the heart of Jesus beheld your heart and loved it."
– For self-donation to the precious love of Jesus, Saint Francis de Sales: ℟

‹ **Saint Alphonsus Liguori** († 1787): "He who does not give up prayer cannot possibly continue to offend God habitually."
– For faithfulness to prayer and deeper spiritual fervor, Saint Alphonsus Liguori: ℟

‹ **Saint Thérèse of Lisieux** († 1897): "What pleases Jesus is that he sees me loving my littleness and my poverty, the blind hope that I have in his mercy."
– For the grace of spiritual childhood, Saint Thérèse of Lisieux: ℟

Blessing to
Receive the Graces of the Most Holy Eucharist

"In the Eucharist we have Jesus, we have his redemptive sacrifice, we have his resurrection, we have the gift of the Holy Spirit, we have adoration, obedience, and love of the Father. Were we to disregard the Eucharist, how could we overcome our own deficiency?"

Blessed John Paul II

LITANY OF THE HOLY EUCHARIST
(Based on Blessed John Paul II's encyclical
Ecclesia de Eucharistia)

℟ **Feed us with your body, Lord.**

‣ The Eucharist stands at the center of the Church's life. ℟

‣ The Eucharist unites heaven and earth. ℟

‣ The Eucharist embraces and permeates all creation. ℟

‣ The gift of the Eucharist does not remain confined to the past. ℟

‣ Those who feed on Christ in the Eucharist need not wait until the hereafter to receive eternal life. ℟

‣ Those who receive the Eucharist possess the first-fruits of future fullness. ℟

‣ In the Eucharist, Christ makes his presence in meal and sacrifice the promise of a humanity renewed by his love. ℟

‹ All who take part in the Eucharist must be committed to changing their lives and making them Eucharistic. ℞

‹ The Church grows as often as the sacrifice of the cross is celebrated on the altar. ℞

‹ Incorporation into Christ is constantly renewed and consolidated by sharing in the Eucharistic sacrifice. ℞

‹ In sacramental communion, Christ receives each of us, entering into friendship with us. ℞

‹ Eucharistic communion brings about in a sublime way the mutual abiding of Christ. ℞

‹ The seeds of disunity so deeply rooted in humanity as a result of sin are countered by the unifying power of the body of Christ. ℞

‹ The worship of the Eucharist outside of the Mass is of inestimable value for the life of the Church. ℞

‹ The mystery of communion is so perfect that it brings us to the heights of every good thing. ℞

‹ Eucharistic communion is the ultimate goal of every human desire. ℞

‹ In Eucharistic communion we attain God and God joins himself to us in the most perfect union. ℞

‹ The Eucharist is the summit of the spiritual life and the goal of all the sacraments. ℞

‹ A truly Eucharistic community cannot be closed in upon itself. ℞

‹ The Eucharist creates communion and fosters communion. ℞

‹ The Eucharist is the self-gift that the divine Bridegroom continually makes to his Bride. ℞

‹ The Bread of angels cannot be approached except with humility. ℞

‹ The Eucharist offers sustenance to individuals and to entire peoples. ℞

‹ The Eucharist shapes cultures inspired by Christianity. ℞

‹ The Blessed Virgin Mary can guide us toward this most holy sacrament. ℞

‹ Mary is a woman of the Eucharist in her whole life. ℞

‹ The Eucharist is a mystery of faith that calls for sheer abandonment to the Word of God. ℞

‹ There is a profound analogy between Mary's *Fiat* and the believer's *Amen* at Holy Communion. ℞

‹ The memorial of Christ's death in the Eucharist means continually receiving the gift of Mary as our Mother. ℞

‹ Gazing upon Mary we come to know the transforming power present in the Eucharist. ℞

‹ The Most Holy Eucharist is the Church's treasure. ℞

‹ The Most Holy Eucharist is the heart of the world. ℞

‹ The Most Holy Eucharist is the pledge of the fulfillment for which each man and woman yearns. ℞

‹ Every commitment to holiness must draw the strength it needs from the Eucharistic mystery. ℞

‹ In this sacrament is recapitulated the whole mystery of our salvation. ℞

‹ In the Eucharist, Christ walks beside us as our strength and our food for the journey. ℞

‹ In the Eucharist, Christ enables us to become for everyone witnesses of hope. ℞

Blessing to
Live in God's Presence

This blessing might be broken down into a number of parts
that can be shared by different members of the family.

WORD OF GOD

SUNDAY

And the Word became flesh/ and made his dwelling among us,/ and we saw his glory,/ the glory as of the Father's only Son,/ full of grace and truth. (Jn 1: 14)

MONDAY

"Behold, the virgin shall be with child and bear a son,/ and they shall name him Emmanuel,"/ which means "God is with us." (Mt 1: 23)

TUESDAY

"For where two or three are gathered together in my name, there am I in the midst of them." (Mt 18: 20)

WEDNESDAY

When the disciples saw [Jesus] walking on the sea they were terrified. "It is a ghost," they said, and they cried out in fear. At once [Jesus] spoke to them, "Take courage, it is I; do not be afraid." (Mt 14: 26-27)

THURSDAY

"Behold, I stand at the door and knock. If anyone hears my voice and opens the door, [then] I will enter his house and dine with him, and he with me." (Rv 3: 20)

FRIDAY

I heard a loud voice from the throne saying, "Behold, God's dwelling is with the human race. He will dwell with them and they will be his people and God himself will always be with them [as their God]." (Rv 21: 3)

SATURDAY

"And behold, I am with you always, until the end of the age." (Mt 28: 20)

LITANY TO GROW IN THE AWARENESS OF GOD'S PRESENCE

℟ Jesus, you are with us always.

‹ When I have doubt about the Mystery who is my destiny, let me remember: ℟

‹ When tempted to turn God into an abstraction or an idea, let me remember: ℟

‹ When I forget how much I depend on an Other for everything in my life, let me remember: ℟

‹ When frustrated by my expectation for happiness and perfection, let me remember: ℟

‹ When I foolishly make my understanding the measure of all things, let me remember: ℟

‹ When I attempt to live without affirming some ultimate "something," let me remember: ℟

‹ When I live without a taste for life, let me remember: ℟

‹ When I am not engaged in every dimension of reality, let me remember: ℟

‹ When I slight the treasure of friendship, let me remember: ℟

‹ When overwhelmed by drudgery, tedium, or fatigue, let me remember: ℞

‹ When I forget that only my relationship with God makes the adventure of life possible, let me remember: ℞

‹ When I fail to be involved seriously with life, with all its events, encounters, and problems, let me remember: ℞

‹ When I forget that within every single gesture lies a step toward my true destiny, let me remember: ℞

‹ When I lack eagerness in my search for the ultimate meaning of life, let me remember: ℞

‹ When I try to explain everything by some idol, let me remember: ℞

‹ When I give in to the stupidity of distraction, let me remember: ℞

‹ When I refuse to commit myself to my whole life, let me remember: ℞

‹ When my "I" loses sight of the divine "You" who alone can fulfill me, let me remember: ℞

‹ When my life becomes hardened, crust-like, or anesthetized, let me remember: ℞

‹ When I live devoid of wonder, let me remember: ℞

‹ When I am unwilling to be provoked by the totality of the event of Christ, let me remember: ℞

‹ When tempted to stop asking the ultimate questions about life's meaning, let me remember: ℞

‹ When I forget that the world is a revelation of God, let me remember: ℞

Closing Prayer

MOST MERCIFUL FATHER, you revealed your saving presence to Noah in the rainbow, to Moses in the burning bush, to the Israelites in the column of cloud and fire, to David in the ark of the covenant, and to the world in the womb of Mary, the Mother of your Son. Draw me close to your nearness, and help me to remember how much you love to reveal the miracle of your presence in the ordinariness of everyday life. I ask you this in the name of Jesus, our Savior and your Son, who is with us always until the end of the world.

Blessing on
Our Efforts to Change

Place before the Lord all those areas of your life in which change is necessary, and ask for the Holy Spirit's gift of courage.

WORD OF GOD

SUNDAY

But our citizenship is in heaven, and from it we also await a savior, the Lord Jesus Christ. He will change our lowly body to conform with his glorified body by the power that enables him also to bring all things into subjection to himself. (Phil 3: 20-21)

MONDAY

He called a child over, placed it in their midst, and said, "Amen, I say to you, unless you turn and become like children, you will not enter the kingdom of heaven." (Mt 18: 2-3)

TUESDAY

Behold, I tell you a mystery. We shall not all fall asleep, but we will all be changed in an instant, in the blink of an eye, at the last trumpet. For the trumpet will sound, the dead will be raised incorruptible, and we shall be changed. (1 Cor 15: 51-52)

WEDNESDAY

All of us, gazing with unveiled face on the glory of the Lord, are being transformed into the same image from glory to glory, as from the Lord who is the Spirit. (2 Cor 3: 18)

THURSDAY

"At the beginning, O Lord, you established the earth,/ and the heavens are the works of your hands./ They will perish, but you remain;/ and they will all grow old like a garment./ You will roll them up like a cloak,/ and like a garment they will be changed./ But you are the same, and your years will have no end." (Heb 1: 10-12)

FRIDAY

"When John came to you in the way of righteousness, you did not believe him; but tax collectors and prostitutes did. Yet even when you saw that, you did not later change your minds and believe him." (Mt 21: 32)

SATURDAY

Do not conform yourselves to this age but be transformed by the renewal of your mind, that you may discern what is the will of God, what is good and pleasing and perfect. (Rom 12: 2)

MEDITATION

"Act up to your light, though in the midst of difficulties, and you will be carried on, you do not know how far. Abraham obeyed the call and journeyed, not knowing whither he went; so we, if we follow the voice of God, shall be brought on step by step into a new world, of which before we had no idea. This is his gracious way with us: he gives, not all at once, but by measure and season, wisely. To him that [have], more shall be given. But we must begin at the beginning. Each truth has its own order; we cannot join the way of life at any point of the course we please; we cannot learn advanced truths before we have learned primary ones."

Blessed John Henry Newman

LITANY OF ABANDONMENT

℟ **Lord, deliver me.**

‹ **From the temptation to give up:** ℟

‹ **From the temptation to disappointment:** ℟

◦ From the temptation to fear and dread: ℞

◦ From the temptation to cynicism: ℞

◦ From the temptation to skepticism: ℞

◦ From the temptation to distrust: ℞

◦ From the temptation to apathy: ℞

◦ From the temptation to obstinacy: ℞

◦ From the temptation to rationalizing: ℞

◦ From the temptation to despondency and despair: ℞

◦ From the temptation to nay-saying: ℞

◦ From the temptation to gloominess: ℞

◦ From the temptation to doubt: ℞

◦ From the temptation to being overly-critical: ℞

◦ From the temptation to indifference: ℞

◦ From the temptation to nihilism: ℞

◦ From the temptation to impatience: ℞

◦ From the temptation to be contrary: ℞

◦ From the temptation to stubbornness: ℞

◦ From the temptation to discouragement: ℞

◦ From the temptation to pessimism: ℞

◦ From the temptation to resignation: ℞

◦ From the temptation to remain stuck in my ways: ℞

◦ From the temptation to dejection: ℞

◦ From the temptation to make excuses: ℞

◦ From the temptation to hopelessness: ℞

◦ From the temptation to defeatism: ℞

- From the temptation to cowardice: ℟
- From the temptation to antagonism: ℟
- From the temptation to rigidity: ℟
- From the temptation to willfulness: ℟
- From the temptation to diffidence: ℟
- From the temptation to anxiety: ℟
- From the temptation to lose heart: ℟
- From the temptation to have an unyielding spirit: ℟
- From the temptation to presumption: ℟
- From the temptation to rash judging: ℟
- From the temptation to obduracy: ℟
- From the temptation to negativity: ℟
- From the temptation to fatalism: ℟

THE SERENITY PRAYER

"GOD GRANT ME the serenity to accept the things I cannot change, courage to change the things I can, and the wisdom to know the difference. Living one day at a time; enjoying one moment at a time; accepting hardship as the pathway to peace. Taking as Jesus did this sinful world as it is, not as I would have it; trusting that he will make all things right if I surrender to his will; that I may be reasonably happy in this life and supremely happy with him for ever in the next."

Reinhold Niebuhr

Blessing on
Our Missionary Vocation

"The universal call to holiness is closely linked to the universal call to mission… To the question, 'Why mission?', we reply… that true liberation consists in opening oneself to the love of Christ."

Blessed John Paul II

Word of God   Jeremiah 1: 5

BEFORE I formed you in the womb I knew you,/ before you were born I dedicated you,/ a prophet to the nations I appointed you.

LITANY OF MISSION
(Based on Blessed John Paul II's encyclical
Redemptoris Missio)

℞ Lord, make me a witness to the nations.

‹ Faith is strengthened when it is given to others. ℞

‹ Missionary activity has but one purpose: to serve man by revealing to him the love of God made manifest in Jesus Christ. ℞

‹ No believer can avoid this supreme duty: to proclaim Christ to all peoples. ℞

‹ The Church's fundamental function in every age is to point the awareness and experience of the whole of humanity toward the mystery of Christ. ℞

‹ The urgency of missionary activity derives from the radical newness of life brought by Christ. ℞

‹ Faith must be offered to the multitudes because they have the right to know the riches of the mystery of Christ. ℟

‹ Mission is an accurate indicator of our faith in Christ and his love for us. ℟

‹ Mission is based, not on human abilities, but on the power of the risen Lord. ℟

‹ Even before activity, mission means witness and a way of life that shines out to others. ℟

‹ The split between the Gospel and culture is undoubtedly the tragedy of our time. ℟

‹ All forms of missionary activity are marked by an awareness that one is furthering human freedom by proclaiming Jesus Christ. ℟

‹ The missionary is convinced that there already exists in individuals an expectation of knowing the truth about God, about man. ℟

‹ Those who have the missionary spirit feel Christ's burning love for souls. ℟

‹ The missionary is a sign of God's love in the world – a love without exclusion or partiality. ℟

‹ The characteristic of every authentic missionary life is the inner joy that comes from faith. ℟

‹ The one who proclaims the "Good News" must be a person who has found true hope in Christ. ℟

Blessing of
Hope

"My hope is in God, who needs not us to accomplish his designs. We must endeavor to be faithful to him and not spoil his work by our shortcomings."

Saint Isaac Jogues, s.j.

Word of God   Psalm 71: 1-6

I N YOU, LORD, I take refuge;/ let me never be put to shame./ In your justice rescue and deliver me;/ listen to me and save me!/ Be my rock and refuge,/ my secure stronghold;/ for you are my rock and fortress./ My God, rescue me from the power of the wicked,/ from the clutches of the violent./ You are my hope, Lord;/ my trust, GOD, from my youth./ On you I depend since birth;/ from my mother's womb you are my strength;/ my hope in you never wavers.

LITANY OF HOPE
(Based on Pope Benedict XVI's encyclical *Spe Salvi*)

℟ **Christ, be my hope.**

‣ Redemption is offered to us in the sense that we have been given trustworthy hope. ℟

‣ By virtue of the hope we have been given, we can face our present. ℟

‣ The present, even if it is arduous, can be lived and accepted if it leads toward a goal great enough to justify the effort of the journey. ℟

‣ A distinguishing mark of Christians is the fact that they have a future. ℟

‹ Christians know that their life will not end in emptiness. ℞

‹ Only when the future is certain as a positive reality does it become possible to live the present as well. ℞

‹ The Gospel is a communication that makes things happen and is life-changing. ℞

‹ To come to know the true God means to receive hope. ℞

‹ Those who live with the Christian concept of God possess the hope that ensues from a real encounter with God. ℞

‹ To have hope means knowing that we are definitively loved and that whatever happens to us, we are awaited by this Love. ℞

‹ Jesus brought an encounter with the living God and thus an encounter with a hope stronger than the suffering of slavery. ℞

‹ Hope transforms life and the world from within. ℞

‹ It is not the laws of matter and evolution that have the final say, but reason, will, love – a Person. ℞

‹ If we know this Person and he knows us, then the inexorable power of material elements no longer has the last word. ℞

‹ If we know this Person and he knows us, we are not slaves of the universe and of its laws – we are free. ℞

‹ Christ tells us who man truly is and what a person must do in order to be truly human. ℞

‹ Christ shows us the way beyond death – and only someone able to do this is a true teacher of life. ℞

‹ The true Shepherd is one who knows even the path that passes through the valley of death. ℞

‹ The true Shepherd walks with me even on the path of final solitude where no one can accompany me, guiding me through. ℞

‹ The true Shepherd has returned to accompany us now and to give us the certainty that, together with him, we can find a way through. ℞

‹ The realization that there is One who even in death accompanies me is the new hope that has arisen over the life of believers. ℞

‹ Through faith there are already present in us the things that are hoped for: the whole, true life. ℞

‹ The presence in us of what is to come creates certainty. ℞

‹ Faith gives us even now something of the reality we are waiting for. ℞

‹ The present reality we experience constitutes for us a "proof" of the things that are still unseen. ℞

‹ Faith draws the future into the present, so that it is no longer simply a "not yet." ℞

‹ The fact that this future exists changes the present. ℞

‹ Faith gives life a new basis, a new foundation on which we can stand. ℞

‹ From the hope of those people who have been touched by Christ, hope has arisen for others who are living in darkness and without hope. ℞

‹ Knowing how to wait, while patiently enduring trials, is necessary for the believer to be able to receive what is promised. ℞

‹ Perseverance and constancy indicate a lived hope – a life based on the certainty of hope. ℞

‹ Hope is the expectation of things to come from the perspective of a present that is already given. ℞

‹ Ultimately we want only one thing – the life which is simply life, simply happiness. ℞

‹ We do not know what we would really like; we do not know this "true life." ℞

‹ We know all the same that there must be something we do not know toward which we feel driven. ℞

‹ In some way, we want life itself, untouched even by death. ℞

‹ We cannot stop reaching out for the thing toward which we feel driven. ℞

‹ We know that all we can experience or accomplish is not what we yearn for. ℞

‹ This unknown "thing" is the true hope which drives us. ℞

‹ To imagine ourselves outside the temporality that imprisons us is like plunging into the ocean of infinite love. ℞

‹ Man needs God, otherwise he remains without hope. ℞

‹ When people have the experience of a great love in their life, this is a moment of "redemption" which gives a new meaning to their life. ℞

‹ If absolute love exists, with its absolute certainty, only then is man "redeemed." ℞

‹ Man's great, true hope which holds firm in spite of all disappointments can only be God who continues to love us to the end. ℞

‹ Whoever is moved by love begins to perceive what "life" really is. ℞

‹ Life in its true sense is not something we have exclusively in or from ourselves: it is a relationship. ℞

‹ If we are in relation with him who does not die, who is Life itself and love itself, then we are in life – then we "live." ℞

‹ Man has need of a hope that goes further than what is finite. ℞

‹ Only something infinite will suffice for the human being – something that will always be more than a person can ever attain. ℞

‹ Truly great hope can only be God who encompasses the whole of reality and who can bestow upon us what we, by ourselves, cannot attain. ℞

‹ God is the foundation of hope – God who has a human face and who has loved us to the end. ℞

‹ God's kingdom is present wherever he is loved and wherever his love reaches us. ℞

‹ God's love alone gives us the possibility of soberly persevering day by day without ceasing to be spurred on by hope. ℞

‹ God's love is our guarantee of the existence of what we await: a life that is "truly" life. ℞

‹ A first essential setting for learning hope is prayer. ℞

‹ When there is no longer anyone to help me deal with a need or expectation that goes beyond the human capacity for hope, God can help me. ℞

‹ All serious and upright human conduct is hope in action. ℞

‹ Believers are enlightened by the radiance of the great hope that cannot be destroyed. ℞

‹ It is important to know that I can always continue to hope, even if in my life there seems to be nothing left to hope for. ℞

‹ Only the great certitude of hope can give one the courage to act and to persevere. ℞

‹ It is the great hope based upon God's promises that gives us courage and directs our action in good times and bad. ℞

‹ It is not by sidestepping or fleeing from suffering that we are healed, but rather by our capacity for accepting it, maturing through it, and finding meaning through union with Christ. ℞

‹ The star of hope has risen – the anchor of the heart reaches the very throne of God. ℟

‹ Suffering – without ceasing to be suffering – becomes, despite everything, a hymn of praise. ℟

‹ Truth and justice must stand above my comfort and physical well-being, or else my life itself becomes a lie. ℟

‹ The capacity to suffer for the sake of the truth is the measure of my humanity. ℟

‹ The capacity to suffer depends on the type and extent of the hope that we bear within us and build upon. ℟

‹ Before Christ's gaze all falsehood melts away. ℟

‹ The encounter with Christ transforms and frees us, allowing us to become truly ourselves. ℟

‹ Our defilement does not stain us for ever if we have at least continued to reach out toward Christ, toward truth, and toward love. ℟

‹ The judgment of God is hope, both because it is justice and because it is grace. ℟

‹ In the communion of souls, it is never too late to touch the heart of another, nor is it ever in vain. ℟

‹ Our hope is essentially also hope for others; only thus is it truly hope for me too. ℟

‹ The true stars of our life are the people who have lived good lives. They are lights of hope. ℟

‹ The Blessed Virgin Mary remains in the midst of Christ's disciples as their Mother, as the Mother of hope. ℟

Blessings and Prayers
for
Special Needs

Blessing for
Those Facing Mental Distress

"We all know that Jesus stood before man in his wholeness in order to heal him completely, in body, mind, and spirit. Indeed, the human person is a unity and his various dimensions can and must be distinguished but not separated. Thus, the Church too always proposes to consider people as such… At this time I am thinking in particular of families with a mentally-ill member who are experiencing the weariness and the various problems that this entails… The Church intends to bow down over those who suffer with special concern, calling the attention of public opinion to the problems connected with mental disturbance that now afflicts one-fifth of humanity and is a real social-health care emergency… I hope that the culture of acceptance and sharing will grow and spread to them… Every Christian, according to his specific duty and responsibility, is called to make his contribution so that the dignity of these brothers and sisters may be recognized, respected, and promoted."

Pope Benedict XVI

Word of God   Philippians 4: 6-7

HAVE NO ANXIETY AT ALL, but in everything, by prayer and petition, with thanksgiving, make your requests known to God. Then the peace of God that surpasses all understanding will guard your hearts and minds in Christ Jesus.

LITANY OF CONSOLATION

‣ When the darkness of depression overshadows me,
– Lord Jesus, you say:
> *I am the Light of the world.*

‹ When plagued by my fragility and all my limitations,

– Lord Jesus, you say:

> *Blessed are the poor in spirit, for theirs is the kingdom of heaven.*

‹ When sadness takes hold of me,

– Lord Jesus, you say:

> *Blessed are those who mourn, for they shall be comforted.*

‹ When tormented by my insecurity and my inadequacy,

– Lord Jesus, you say:

> *Blessed are the meek, for they shall inherit the earth.*

‹ When lost and unsure about where to turn,

– Lord Jesus, you say:

> *Your Father knows what you need before you ask him.*

‹ When fretful and obsessive about so many things,

– Lord Jesus, you say:

> *Do not be anxious about your life, what you shall eat or what you shall drink.*

‹ When lethargy and listlessness take over

– Lord Jesus, you say:

> *Seek first his kingdom and his righteousness, and all these things shall be yours as well.*

‹ When worry about the future paralyzes me,

– Lord Jesus, you say:

> *Let the day's own trouble be sufficient for the day.*

‹ When I feel helpless and forsaken,

– Lord Jesus, you say:

> *Whatever you ask in prayer, you will receive.*

‹ When shame and guilt overwhelm me,

– Lord Jesus, you say:

> *For I came not to call the righteous, but sinners.*

‹ When engulfed by anxiety and fear,

– Lord Jesus, you say:

    Take heart, it is I; have no fear.

‹ When my life lacks any purpose or direction,

– Lord Jesus, you say:

    Follow me.

‹ When I believe I am worthless and a total disappointment,

– Lord Jesus, you say:

    You are of more value than many sparrows.

‹ When weighed down by the addictions of my life,

– Lord Jesus, you say:

    Come to me, all who labor and are heavy laden.

‹ When the harshness and ruthlessness of life assail me,

– Lord Jesus, you say:

    I am gentle and lowly in heart, and you will find rest for your souls.

‹ When it seems I have only a little to offer,

– Lord Jesus, you say:

    To him who has will more be given.

‹ When I crave approval and fear the judgment of others,

 – Lord Jesus, you say:

    Whoever humbles himself like this child, he is the greatest in the kingdom of heaven.

‹ When I'm feeling discouraged because of my body,

– Lord Jesus, you say:

    Abide in me.

‹ When my situation seems hopeless,

– Lord Jesus, you say:

    With God all things are possible.

‹ When I fear that my life is irrelevant and insignificant,

– Lord Jesus, you say:

    But many that are first will be last, and the last first.

‹ When I'm afraid to face the truth about myself,
– Lord Jesus, you say:
> *Whoever humbles himself will be exalted.*

‹ When exhausted by tedium, tiresomeness, and stress,
– Lord Jesus, you say:
> *Come away by yourselves to a lonely place, and rest a while.*

‹ When terrified by the raging storms of life,
– Lord Jesus, you say:
> *Do not be afraid.*

‹ When I am full of doubt, with no one to depend on,
– Lord Jesus, you say:
> *All things are possible to him who believes.*

‹ When it's hard to persevere and I'm tempted to give up,
– Lord Jesus, you say:
> *By your endurance you will gain your lives.*

‹ When bitterness and resentment poison my heart,
– Lord Jesus, you say:
> *If the Son makes you free, you will be free indeed.*

‹ When I feel like I belong to no one,
– Lord Jesus, you say:
> *I am the good shepherd; I know my own and my own know me.*

‹ When I see nothing but my wrongdoing and failures,
– Lord Jesus, you say:
> *Let not your hearts be troubled; believe in me.*

‹ When swayed by moralism, relativism, and nihilism,
– Lord Jesus, you say:
> *I am the way, and the truth, and the life.*

‹ When I'm feeling cut off, alienated, and alone,
– Lord Jesus, you say:
> *I am the vine, you are the branches.*

‹ When duped by self-absorption and self-obsessiveness,
– Lord Jesus, you say:
>*Apart from me you can do nothing.*

‹ When despairing because of isolation and alienation,
– Lord Jesus, you say:
>*I will not leave you desolate; I will come to you.*

‹ When downcast from feeling friendless and betrayed,
– Lord Jesus, you say:
>*I have called you friends.*

‹ When I refuse to believe that anyone could love me,
– Lord Jesus, you say:
>*You did not choose me, but I chose you.*

‹ When tempted to apathy, cynicism, and dread,
– Lord Jesus, you say:
>*Ask, and you will receive, that your joy may be full.*

‹ When polluted by the hatred and violence of the world,
– Lord Jesus, you say:
>*Be of good cheer, I have overcome the world.*

‹ When I think that happiness is nothing but a delusion,
– Lord Jesus, you ask me:
>*Do you love me?*

‹ When my life reaches a dead-end and I lack all desire,
– Lord Jesus, you ask me:
>*Do you love me?*

‹ When I decide that life has no meaning,
– Lord Jesus, you ask me:
>*Do you love me?*

‹ Yes, Lord Jesus, I do!
– Lord Jesus, you say:
>*Abide in my love.*

Blessing for
Those Who Are Suffering

*Write down on slips of paper the names of those
who are suffering, and place them
before a crucifix or an image of our Lord,
the Blessed Mother, or one of the saints.*

Word of God   **2 Corinthians 1: 3-5**

BLESSED BE THE GOD and Father of our Lord Jesus Christ, the Father of compassion and God of all encouragement, who encourages us in our every affliction, so that we may be able to encourage those who are in any affliction with the encouragement with which we ourselves are encouraged by God. For as Christ's sufferings overflow to us, so through Christ does our encouragement also overflow.

LITANY OF INTERCESSION

℞ **Lord, have mercy.**

‣ **For those who suffer because of the death of a loved one:** ℞

‣ **For those who suffer because of sickness, injury, or disability:** ℞

‣ **For those who suffer because of religious persecution:** ℞

‣ **For those who suffer because of addiction:** ℞

‣ **For those who suffer because of old age or incapacitation:** ℞

‣ **For those who suffer because they are not understood:** ℞

‣ **For those who suffer because of pain:** ℞

‣ **For those who suffer because of need, hunger, or poverty:** ℞

‹ For those who suffer because of the tyranny of sin: ℟

‹ For those who suffer because of catastrophes or natural disasters: ℟

‹ For those who suffer because of toilsome work and degrading jobs: ℟

‹ For those who suffer because of being neglected, overlooked, or underappreciated: ℟

‹ For those who suffer because of a broken heart: ℟

‹ For those who suffer because of ignorance or lack of education: ℟

‹ For those who suffer because of bad memories, resentment, or guilt: ℟

‹ For those who suffer because of mockery, ridicule, or humiliation: ℟

‹ For those who suffer because of abuse: ℟

‹ For those who suffer because of injustice or oppression: ℟

‹ For those who suffer because of prejudice, discrimination, racism, or marginalization: ℟

‹ For those who suffer because of violence, cruelty, hatred, or war: ℟

‹ For those who suffer because of homelessness, displacement, or incarceration: ℟

‹ For couples who suffer because they are not able to have children: ℟

‹ For those who suffer because of remorse, depression, anxiety, or mental anguish: ℟

‹ For those who suffer because of rejection or abandonment: ℟

‹ For those who suffer because of unemployment: ℟

‹ For those who suffer because of failure: ℟

‹ For those who suffer because of loneliness: ℟

‹ For those who suffer because of the feeling of being worthless or unwanted: ℟

‹ For parents who suffer because of the loss of a child: ℟

‹ For those who suffer because of any affliction: ℟

‹ For those who suffer because of betrayal: ℟

Blessing in the
Face of Fear

"Do not be afraid because great courage is required if we are to open the doors to Christ, if we are to let Christ enter into our hearts... Do not be afraid! If you begin to lose courage, turn to Mary, seat of wisdom; with her at your side, you will never be afraid."

Blessed John Paul II

WORD OF GOD

SUNDAY

For those who are led by the Spirit of God are children of God. For you did not receive a spirit of slavery to fall back into fear, but you received a spirit of adoption, through which we cry, "*Abba*, Father!" (Rom 8: 14-15)

MONDAY

Now since the children share in blood and flesh, he likewise shared in them, that through death he might destroy the one who has the power of death, that is, the devil, and free those who through fear of death had been subject to slavery all their life. (Heb 2: 14-15)

TUESDAY

There is no fear in love, but perfect love drives out fear because fear has to do with punishment, and so one who fears is not yet perfect in love. (1 Jn 4: 18)

WEDNESDAY

When I caught sight of him, I fell down at his feet as though dead. He touched me with his right hand and said, "Do not be afraid.

I am the first and the last, the one who lives. Once I was dead, but now I am alive forever and ever. I hold the keys to death and the netherworld." (Rv 1: 17-18)

THURSDAY

Thus we may say with confidence:/ "The Lord is my helper,/ [and] I will not be afraid./ What can anyone do to me?" (Heb 13: 6)

FRIDAY

Now who is going to harm you if you are enthusiastic for what is good? But even if you should suffer because of righteousness, blessed are you. Do not be afraid or terrified with fear of them, but sanctify Christ as Lord in your hearts. Always be ready to give an explanation to anyone who asks you for a reason for your hope. (1 Pt 3: 13-15)

SATURDAY

"Do not be afraid of anything that you are going to suffer. Indeed, the devil will throw some of you into prison, that you may be tested, and you will face an ordeal for ten days. Remain faithful until death, and I will give you the crown of life." (Rv 2: 10)

LITANY TO OVERCOME FEAR

℟ **Lord, deliver me.**

• From the fear of suffering: ℟

• From the fear of pain: ℟

• From the fear of failure: ℟

• From the fear of inferiority: ℟

• From the fear of abandonment: ℟

• From the fear of things that are new: ℟

‹ From the fear of losing loved ones: ℟

‹ From the fear of violence: ℟

‹ From the fear of not being able to cope: ℟

‹ From the fear of being myself: ℟

‹ From the fear of loss of health: ℟

‹ From the fear of growing old: ℟

‹ From the fear of bodily harm: ℟

‹ From the fear of disasters: ℟

‹ From the fear of being alone: ℟

‹ From the fear of not being liked: ℟

‹ From the fear of betrayal: ℟

‹ From the fear of being laughed at: ℟

‹ From the fear of disgrace: ℟

‹ From the fear of loneliness: ℟

‹ From the fear of being used: ℟

‹ From the fear of rejection: ℟

‹ From the fear of the future: ℟

‹ From the fear of embarrassment: ℟

‹ From the fear of shame: ℟

‹ From the fear of being inadequate: ℟

‹ From the fear of ridicule: ℟

‹ From the fear of change: ℟

‹ From the fear of humiliation: ℟

‹ From the fear of facing my secret sins: ℟

- From the fear of judgment by others: ℟
- From the fear of darkness: ℟
- From the fear of silence: ℟
- From the fear of being poor: ℟
- From the fear of financial insecurity: ℟
- From the fear of defeat: ℟
- From the fear of criticism: ℟
- From the fear of disappointing others: ℟
- From the fear of not being loved enough: ℟
- From the fear of isolation: ℟
- From the fear of powerlessness: ℟
- From the irrational fear of punishment: ℟
- From the fear of what others think of me: ℟
- From the fear aroused by things in the past: ℟
- From the fear of terrorism: ℟
- From the fear of the unknown: ℟
- From the fear of witnessing to my faith: ℟
- From the fear of being forsaken: ℟
- From the fear of death: ℟
- From all fears that enslave: ℟
- From all phobias: ℟
- From the fear of not doing God's will: ℟

Prayer for
Those Who Are Sick

WORD OF GOD

SUNDAY

"Come to me, all you who labor and are burdened, and I will give you rest. Take my yoke upon you and learn from me, for I am meek and humble of heart; and you will find rest for yourselves. For my yoke is easy, and my burden light." (Mt 11: 28-30)

MONDAY

Three times I begged the Lord about this, that it might leave me, but he said to me, "My grace is sufficient for you, for power is made perfect in weakness." I will rather boast most gladly of my weaknesses, in order that the power of Christ may dwell with me. Therefore, I am content with weaknesses, insults, hardships, persecutions, and constraints, for the sake of Christ; for when I am weak, then I am strong. (2 Cor 12: 8-10)

TUESDAY

I consider that the sufferings of this present time are as nothing compared with the glory to be revealed for us. We know that all creation is groaning in labor pains even until now. But if we hope for what we do not see, we wait with endurance. (Rom 8: 18, 22, 25)

WEDNESDAY

For indeed he was crucified out of weakness, but he lives by the power of God. So also we are weak in him, but toward you we shall live with him by the power of God. (2 Cor 13: 4)

THURSDAY

For through the law I died to the law, that I might live for God. I have been crucified with Christ; yet I live, no longer I, but Christ lives in me; insofar as I now live in the flesh, I live by faith in the Son of God who has loved me and given himself up for me. (Gal 2: 19-20)

Friday

For to this you have been called, because Christ also suffered for you, leaving you an example that you should follow in his footsteps./ "He committed no sin,/ and no deceit was found in his mouth."/ When he was insulted, he returned no insult; when he suffered, he did not threaten; instead, he handed himself over to the one who judges justly. He himself bore our sins in his body upon the cross, so that, free from sin, we might live for righteousness. By his wounds you have been healed. (1 Pt 2: 21-24)

Saturday

Blessed be the God and Father of our Lord Jesus Christ, the Father of compassion and God of all encouragement, who encourages us in our every affliction, so that we may be able to encourage those who are in any affliction with the encouragement with which we ourselves are encouraged by God. For as Christ's sufferings overflow to us, so through Christ does our encouragement also overflow. If we are afflicted, it is for your encouragement and salvation; if we are encouraged, it is for your encouragement, which enables you to endure the same sufferings that we suffer. Our hope for you is firm, for we know that as you share in the sufferings, you also share in the encouragement. (2 Cor 1: 3-7)

Litany of Compassion for the Sick

We pray with special love and concern for all those who are ill or infirm, asking the Lord for his consoling grace to strengthen the sick in times of trial.

℟ **Lord, be close to give your comfort.**

‣ When pain or distress is overwhelming: ℟

‹ When the healing process goes slower than hoped: ℞

‹ When terrified by treatments or therapy: ℞

‹ When it's hard to let go of long-held plans: ℞

‹ When the feeling of alienation arises: ℞

‹ When worn out and weary: ℞

‹ When troubled by impatience and negativity: ℞

‹ When loneliness adds to anxiety: ℞

‹ When sickness makes it difficult to communicate: ℞

‹ When discouragement or despondency sets in: ℞

‹ When fear makes it impossible to face the future: ℞

‹ When the ravages of disease attack self-esteem: ℞

‹ When anger and resentment assail: ℞

‹ When beset by worry or fretfulness: ℞

‹ When it's hard to rely on others for care: ℞

‹ When envy arises toward those who are healthy: ℞

‹ When pessimism or cynicism holds sway: ℞

‹ When anguish is intensified by the need for reconciliation: ℞

‹ When sickness is mistaken for punishment: ℞

‹ When loved ones are far away: ℞

‹ When sickness causes financial hardship that leads to worry or despair: ℞

‹ When afflicted by the feeling of nothing to hope for: ℞

‹ When weakness makes it impossible even to think: ℞

‹ When friends draw back, fearful of disease: ℞

‹ When illness makes those who are suffering moody or irritable: ℞

‹ When haunted by regret and the shame of past sins: ℟

‹ When it's difficult to sleep: ℟

‹ When there's loss of appetite: ℟

‹ When there's resistance to necessary change: ℟

‹ When tempted by denial: ℟

‹ When nobody seems to understand: ℟

‹ When bound to home or when restricted in movement: ℟

‹ When listlessness and apathy threaten: ℟

‹ When medication seems to make things worse: ℟

‹ When all that's needed is a caring touch: ℟

‹ When it's impossible to maintain familiar routines: ℟

‹ When it's hard to find the strength to go on: ℟

‹ When it becomes difficult to pray: ℟

‹ When suffering of any sort becomes hard to bear: ℟

‹ When death draws near: ℟

CLOSING PRAYER

MOST MERCIFUL FATHER, your beloved Son showed special compassion to lepers, tenderness to those long sick, and healing to the infirm laid before him. We place before you all those who are ill and in need of healing grace. May the love and mercy of the Divine Physician raise up all who suffer from sickness and restore them to health and peace. We ask this in the name of Jesus.

Blessing on
Making a New Beginning

Place before the Lord all the new beginnings of your life,
especially those that cause anxiety or fear.

Word of God   Revelation 21: 6-7

I [AM] THE ALPHA AND THE OMEGA, the beginning and the end. To the thirsty I will give a gift from the spring of life-giving water. The victor will inherit these gifts, and I shall be his God, and he will be my son.

LITANY FOR NEW BEGINNINGS

Saint Gregory of Nyssa wrote that "he who climbs never stops going from beginning to beginning, through beginnings that have no end. He never stops desiring what he already knows." Imbued with this truth, we ask the Lord to give us the strength to begin anew and to bless all new beginnings as we pray: Lord, pour out your Spirit.

℟ **Lord, pour out your Spirit.**

‣ On recent graduates: ℟

‣ On newlyweds: ℟

‣ On those who have moved to a new home: ℟

‣ On those starting new jobs: ℟

‣ On those with new families: ℟

‣ On those facing new challenges: ℟

‣ On those living away from home for the first time: ℟

‣ On those who have just become sick: ℟

‹ On those assuming new authority: ℟

‹ On those turning over a new leaf: ℟

‹ On newly pregnant mothers: ℟

‹ On newborn children: ℟

‹ On those newly forgiven: ℟

‹ On those beginning retirement: ℟

‹ On those in recovery: ℟

‹ On new friendships: ℟

‹ On those released from prison: ℟

‹ On those beginning a new career: ℟

‹ On those starting a new grade in school: ℟

‹ On those newly returned to health: ℟

‹ On those faced with new responsibilities: ℟

‹ On those who have been offered a second chance: ℟

‹ On those committed to new resolutions: ℟

‹ On those who make laws and protect the common good: ℟

‹ On those afraid to risk or trust: ℟

‹ On those dedicated to self-improvement: ℟

‹ On those with new burdens or sufferings: ℟

‹ On all new beginnings: ℟

‹ On this day: ℟

Closing Prayer

LORD JESUS, in the beginning was the Word. You are the saving Word of God. You are the beginning, the first-born of the dead. Absolute fullness resides in you. You alone have the power to reconcile everything and to make peace by the blood of your cross. We are creatures who are not our own beginning. Help us to welcome every new beginning with courage and grace. Fill us with your presence so that we may never stop going from beginning to beginning so as to reach you in the holiness of faith, for you are our Lord, now and for ever.

Blessing on
Those Far from Home

We lift up to the Lord all those who are separated from us by distance and ask the Lord to bless and protect them.

Confident in the closeness of the Lord, we pray for those who are physically far away that they may know the intimacy and consolation of Christ's saving presence.

WORD OF GOD

SUNDAY

"For the promise is made to you and to your children and to all those far off, whomever the Lord our God will call." (Acts 2: 39)

MONDAY

Hear, you who are far off, what I have done;/ you who are near, acknowledge my might. (Is 33: 13)

TUESDAY

Distant peoples stand in awe of your marvels;/ east and west you make resound with joy. (Ps 65: 9)

WEDNESDAY

Peace, peace to the far and the near,/ says the LORD; and I will heal them. (Is 57: 19)

THURSDAY

You whom I have taken from the ends of the earth/ and summoned from its far-off places,/ You whom I have called my servant,/ whom I have chosen and will not cast off –/ Fear not, I am with you. (Is 41: 9-10a)

Friday

But now in Christ Jesus you who once were far off have become near by the blood of Christ. (Eph 2: 13)

Saturday

[Jesus] came and preached peace to you who were far off and peace to those who were near, for through him we both have access in one Spirit to the Father. (Eph 2: 17-18)

Litany for Those Far from Us

℟ **Lord, protect them by your mercy.**

‣ For families separated by distance: ℟

‣ For those serving abroad in the military: ℟

‣ For refugees: ℟

‣ For those who are ill and in the hospital: ℟

‣ For those away at school: ℟

‣ For those who are missing: ℟

‣ For those away at work: ℟

‣ For those in prison: ℟

‣ For those confined to nursing homes: ℟

‣ For those who are traveling: ℟

‣ For those living abroad: ℟

‣ For those separated by conflict or turmoil: ℟

‣ For those made lonely by distance or solitude: ℟

‣ For all those far from the ones they love: ℟

Closing Prayer

MOST MERCIFUL FATHER, the night before he died your beloved Son prayed that we might share the unity that Jesus our Savior shares with you. In the moments when we are far from those we love, may Christ's prayer be our comfort and our confidence. In our times of separation may we know your love living in us through the presence of Jesus living in us. Jesus "is always able to save those who approach God through him, since he lives forever to make intercession for them" (Heb 7: 25). We approach him now in faith so that we may come close in love to those we love so far from us. Bless, protect them, and keep them safe in your grace. We ask this through Christ our Lord.

Blessing to
Sanctify Work

"Work is not only good in the sense that it is useful or something to enjoy; it is also good as being something worthy, that is to say, something that corresponds to man's dignity, that expresses this dignity and increases it… Work is a good thing for man – a good thing for his humanity – because through work man not only transforms nature, adapting it to his own needs, but he also achieves fulfillment as a human being and indeed in a sense becomes 'more a human being.'"

Blessed John Paul II

Word of God

Sunday

Jesus said to them, "My food is to do the will of the one who sent me and to finish his work. My Father is at work until now, so I am at work. Do not work for food that perishes but for the food that endures for eternal life, which the Son of Man will give you. For on him the Father, God, has set his seal." (Jn 4: 34; 5: 17; 6: 27)

Monday

"Who among you would say to your servant who has just come in from plowing or tending sheep in the field, 'Come here immediately and take your place at table'? Would he not rather say to him, 'Prepare something for me to eat. Put on your apron and wait on me while I eat and drink. You may eat and drink when I am finished'? Is he grateful to that servant because he did what was commanded? So should it be with you. When you have done all you have been commanded, say,

'We are unprofitable servants; we have done what we were obliged to do.'" (Lk 17: 7-10)

TUESDAY

The thief must no longer steal, but rather labor, doing honest work with his [own] hands, so that he may have something to share with one in need. (Eph 4: 28)

WEDNESDAY

So then, my beloved, obedient as you have always been, not only when I am present but all the more now when I am absent, work out your salvation with fear and trembling. For God is the one who, for his good purpose, works in you both to desire and to work. Do everything without grumbling or questioning. (Phil 2: 12-14)

THURSDAY

We urge you, brothers, to progress even more, and to aspire to live a tranquil life, to mind your own affairs, and to work with your [own] hands, as we instructed you. (1 Thes 4: 10b-11)

FRIDAY

In fact, when we were with you, we instructed you that if anyone was unwilling to work, neither should that one eat. We hear that some are conducting themselves among you in a disorderly way, by not keeping busy but minding the business of others. Such people we instruct and urge in the Lord Jesus Christ to work quietly and to eat their own food. (2 Thes 3: 10-12)

SATURDAY

"Blessed are those servants whom the master finds vigilant on his arrival. Amen, I say to you, he will gird himself, have them recline at table, and proceed to wait on them." (Lk 12: 37)

MEDITATION

"The Christian finds in human work a small part of the cross of Christ and accepts it in the same spirit of redemption in which Christ accepted the cross for us. In work, thanks to the light that penetrates us from the Resurrection of Christ, we always find a glimmer of new life, of the new good, as if it were an announcement of 'the new heavens and the new earth' in which man and the world participate precisely through the toil that goes with work."

Blessed John Paul II

LITANY TO SANCTIFY WORK

In a spirit of sacrifice, we consecrate our workday to the Lord and pray:

℟ Lord, protect me.

‹ From the temptation to be listless and lazy: ℟

‹ From the temptation to complain: ℟

‹ From the temptation to be critical of my boss: ℟

‹ From the temptation to cheat or to be dishonest with others: ℟

‹ From the temptation to gossip: ℟

‹ From the temptation to lateness: ℟

‹ From the temptation to waste time: ℟

‹ From the temptation to be judgmental of my co-workers: ℟

‹ From the temptation to procrastinate: ℟

‹ From the temptation to be jealous or envious of others: ℟

‹ From the temptation to indolence and lethargy: ℟

‹ From the temptation to be hyper-critical: ℟

‹ From the temptation to engage in idle conversation: ℟

- From the temptation to be quick to take offense: ℟
- From the temptation to shift my work onto others: ℟
- From the temptation to impatience: ℟
- From the temptation to cut corners or to be sloppy: ℟
- From the temptation to give in to weariness: ℟

℟ Lord, please grant it.

- For the grace to be a peacemaker: ℟
- For the grace to witness to you by word and example: ℟
- For the grace to be energetic and committed: ℟
- For the grace to be compassionate and forgiving: ℟
- For the grace to offer up all tedium and drudgery: ℟
- For the grace to be attentive to those in need: ℟
- For the grace to be generous in sharing: ℟
- For the grace to be prudent in dealing with others: ℟
- For the grace to be kind: ℟
- For the grace to be understanding: ℟
- For the grace to fulfill my responsibilities well: ℟
- For the grace to be patient and persevering: ℟
- For the grace to put myself in others' shoes: ℟
- For the grace to be dedicated and undistracted: ℟
- For the grace to be honest and forthright: ℟
- For the grace to be hard-working: ℟
- For the grace to be free of stress: ℟
- For the grace of insight to solve problems: ℟
- For the grace of industriousness: ℟

‹ For the grace to resolve conflicts and difficulties: ℟

‹ For the grace to put up with hardships: ℟

‹ For the grace to esteem the dignity of my co-workers: ℟

‹ For the grace to be thankful for the chance to work: ℟

‹ For the grace to spread the good news of the Gospel: ℟

PRAYER AFTER WORK

MOST MERCIFUL FATHER, thank you for this day of work with all its achievements as well as its burdens. Thank you for all the successes, the challenges, and even the difficulties that it brought me. Your Son once said to his apostles, "Come by yourselves to an out-of-the-way place and rest a little." Thank you for this gift of rest. May this time be a chance for me to renew my gratitude for all your blessings. In your great compassion and generosity, please be mindful of those who are out of work. And help me to do a better job tomorrow. I ask this through Christ our Lord.

Blessing to
Heal Past Hurts

"In suffering there is concealed a particular power that draws a person interiorly close to Christ... Suffering, more than anything else, makes present... the powers of the Redemption... Suffering is present in the world in order to release love."

Blessed John Paul II

WORD OF GOD

SUNDAY

"Come to me, all you who labor and are burdened, and I will give you rest. Take my yoke upon you and learn from me, for I am meek and humble of heart; and you will find rest for yourselves. For my yoke is easy, and my burden light." (Mt 11: 28-30)

MONDAY

[We are] always carrying about in the body the dying of Jesus, so that the life of Jesus may also be manifested in our body. For we who live are constantly being given up to death for the sake of Jesus, so that the life of Jesus may be manifested in our mortal flesh. So death is at work in us, but life in you. (2 Cor 4: 10-12)

TUESDAY

But rejoice to the extent that you share in the sufferings of Christ, so that when his glory is revealed you may also rejoice exultantly. If you are insulted for the name of Christ, blessed are you, for the Spirit of glory and of God rests upon you. (1 Pt 4: 13-14)

WEDNESDAY

"If you forgive others their transgressions, your heavenly Father will forgive you. But if you do not forgive others, neither will your Father forgive your transgressions." (Mt 6: 14-15)

THURSDAY

[The] God of all encouragement [...] encourages us in our every affliction, so that we may be able to encourage those who are in any affliction with the encouragement with which we ourselves are encouraged by God. For as Christ's sufferings overflow to us, so through Christ does our encouragement also overflow. (2 Cor 1: 3b-5)

FRIDAY

The God of all grace, who called you to his eternal glory through Christ [Jesus] will himself restore, confirm, strengthen, and establish you after you have suffered a little. (1 Pt 5: 10)

SATURDAY

A leper came to [Jesus] [and kneeling down] begged him and said, "If you wish, you can make me clean." Moved with pity, he stretched out his hand, touched him, and said to him, "I do will it. Be made clean." (Mk 1: 40-41)

LITANY FOR THE HEALING OF PAST HURTS

℟ **Lord, by your wounds, heal them.**

‣ For the victims of terrorism: ℟

‣ For the grief-stricken and bereaved: ℟

‣ For those overcome by anger and rage: ℟

‣ For the broken-hearted: ℟

‹ For those lost in confusion and despondency: ℟

‹ For those besieged by bitterness and resentment: ℟

‹ For those who live in fear and dread: ℟

‹ For those enslaved by vindictiveness: ℟

‹ For those distraught at the death of one who died young: ℟

‹ For those held captive by the refusal to forgive: ℟

‹ For those broken by injustice: ℟

‹ For those suffering from physical or psychological violence: ℟

‹ For those obsessed with grudges: ℟

‹ For those who have been abused: ℟

‹ For those afflicted by slander, detraction, or calumny: ℟

‹ For those troubled by a lack of recognition: ℟

‹ For those who have been robbed or burglarized: ℟

‹ For those who feel betrayed: ℟

‹ For the victims of oppression: ℟

‹ For those who refuse to forgive themselves: ℟

‹ For those suffering from broken homes: ℟

‹ For those scarred by prejudice and discrimination: ℟

‹ For those in anguish because of abandonment or neglect: ℟

‹ For those who have been cheated or deceived: ℟

‹ For those tormented by bad memories: ℟

‹ For those consumed by the desire for revenge: ℟

‹ For those on the verge of despair: ℟

‹ For those who blame themselves for things beyond their control: ℟

‹ For all those with hurts from the past still in need of healing: ℟

CLOSING PRAYER

LORD JESUS, the only way to true happiness is by passing through your holy cross. Unite my pain with the sufferings of your Passion, and by that union heal me and all those who suffer due to hurts of the past. Help me to know the tenderness of your presence and the power of divine providence in all of life's agonies and afflictions. For you are the Lord of all, now and for ever.

Prayer for
a Happy Death

"Oh, the dullness and hardness of a heart that looks only to the present instead of preparing for that which is to come! Therefore, in every deed and every thought, act as though you were to die this very day. If you had a good conscience you would not fear death very much. It is better to avoid sin than to fear death."

Venerable Thomas à Kempis

WORD OF GOD

SUNDAY

Now since the children share in blood and flesh, he likewise shared in them, that through death he might destroy the one who has the power of death, that is, the devil, and free those who through fear of death had been subject to slavery all their life. (Heb 2: 14-15)

MONDAY

We were indeed buried with him through baptism into death, so that, just as Christ was raised from the dead by the glory of the Father, we too might live in newness of life.
For if we have grown into union with him through a death like his, we shall also be united with him in the resurrection. (Rom 6: 4-5)

TUESDAY

For I am convinced that neither death, nor life, nor angels, nor principalities, nor present things, nor future things, nor powers, nor height, nor depth, nor any other creature will be able to separate us from the love of God in Christ Jesus our Lord. (Rom 8: 38-39)

WEDNESDAY

Every day I face death; I swear it by the pride in you [brothers] that I have in Christ Jesus our Lord. (1 Cor 15: 31)

THURSDAY

For we who live are constantly being given up to death for the sake of Jesus, so that the life of Jesus may be manifested in our mortal flesh. (2 Cor 4: 11)

FRIDAY

My eager expectation and hope is that I shall not be put to shame in any way, but that with all boldness, now as always, Christ will be magnified in my body, whether by life or by death. For to me life is Christ, and death is gain. (Phil 1: 20-21)

SATURDAY

Put to death, then, the parts of you that are earthly: immorality, impurity, passion, evil desire, and the greed that is idolatry. (Col 3: 5)

MEDITATION

"My Savior, grant that the arduous task of my salvation may be brought to a happy conclusion. May neither the lashing rains, nor the impetus of torrents racing down from the mountains, nor the violent storm be able to shake my house. With your victorious hand, assist me, Lord! Be my help, preserve my life, that I may praise you, the giver and Lord of all that is most precious and the salvation of men. Without you, Almighty, no work would exist, no project, no idea, no proposal, no security, nor any of those things that would serve to attain the final end. You have created and given me both soul and body; you have raised me up when I had fallen, and have shown me the way to heaven. And you will bring me in, without merit of mine, to your house to live with you in eternity and to sing a hymn to your glory along with all the blessed."

Saint Maximus the Confessor

LITANY FOR THE HOLY SOULS

℟ **Lord, have mercy.**

ᴕ For those who have died without asking for forgiveness: ℟

ᴕ For those who have died filled with anger: ℟

ᴕ For those who have died spurning prayer: ℟

ᴕ For those who have died without forgiving others: ℟

ᴕ For those who have died filled with obstinacy: ℟

ᴕ For those who have died hating their enemies: ℟

ᴕ For those who have died neglecting their faith: ℟

ᴕ For those who have died rife with resentment: ℟

ᴕ For those who have died without ever saying, "I'm sorry": ℟

ᴕ For those who have died not needing anyone else: ℟

ᴕ For those who have died given over to defiance or rebellion: ℟

ᴕ For those who have died in love with arrogance: ℟

ᴕ For those who have died enslaved to egoism or individualism: ℟

ᴕ For those who have died imbued with bitterness: ℟

ᴕ For those who have died attached to worldly pleasures and indulgence: ℟

ᴕ For those who have died oblivious to the poor and the needy: ℟

ᴕ For those who have died bloated with self-love: ℟

- For those who have died indignant and self-righteous: ℟
- For those who have died ungrateful and ungiving: ℟
- For those who have died dejected and defeated: ℟
- For those who have died smug and self-important: ℟
- For those who have died disheartened and disgruntled: ℟
- For those who have died longing for reconciliation: ℟
- For those who have died tormented by regrets: ℟
- For those who have died with disdain for purity: ℟
- For those who have died with a vengeful or spiteful spirit: ℟
- For those who have died with indifference toward holiness: ℟
- For those who have died with unconverted desires: ℟
- For those who have died isolated or alienated: ℟
- For those who have died unresponsive to God's friendship: ℟
- For those who have died infatuated with self-satisfaction: ℟
- For those who have died surrounded by false idols: ℟
- For those who have died obsessed with avarice: ℟
- For those who have died cold and hard-hearted: ℟
- For those who have died cynical and skeptical: ℟
- For those who have died disappointed and hurt: ℟
- For those who have died suddenly or violently: ℟
- For those who have died without being prepared: ℟
- For those who have died dismissive of the power of grace: ℟
- For those who have died deaf to God's Word: ℟
- For those who have died without ever saying "I love you": ℟

‣ For those who have died without the benefit of the sacraments: ℟

‣ For those who have died who have not sufficiently expiated their faults: ℟

‣ For those who have died lost in their sin: ℟

‣ For those who have died yearning for divine mercy: ℟

‣ For those who have died with the hope of eternal salvation: ℟

CLOSING PRAYER

MOST MERCIFUL FATHER, your beloved Son Jesus reached out with compassion to the widow of Nain and restored her dead son to life. By his Resurrection, Christ has conquered death. Fill me with confidence and trust in our Savior's compassion. May I face death without fear, and live with unwavering hope in the One who raised Lazarus from the dead. For Jesus is our Lord, now and for ever.

Acknowledgments

Page 24: *Directory on Popular Piety and the Liturgy*, 108, Principles and Guidelines. Used with permission of the Libreria Editrice Vaticana. www.vatican.va.

Page 28: Pope Benedict XVI, *Message for Lent 2006*. Used with permission of the Libreria Editrice Vaticana. www.vatican.va.

Page 38: Saint Gregory of Nazianzen, *Observing Holy Week*. © The Crossroads Initiative. www.crossroadsinitiative.com.

Page 50: Blessed John Paul II, *Gift and Mystery*. © 1996, Random House, Inc., New York, NY. Libreria Editrice Vaticana. www.vatican.va. Used with permission.

Page 56: *Directory on Popular Piety and the Liturgy*, 169, Principles and Guidelines. Used with permission of the Libreria Editrice Vaticana. www.vatican.va.

Page 60: Saint Augustine *Sermons*, The Works of Saint Augustine, III/10, John E. Rotelle, O.S.A., Ed., Edmund Hill, O.P., Tr. © 1995, Augustinian Heritage Institute, New City Press. Used with permission.

Page 60: Rose Hawthorne Lathrop (Mother Alphonsa), *Rose Hawthorne Lathrop*, edited by Diana Culbertson, O.P. © 1993, Diana Culbertson, O.P. Paulist Press, Inc., New York/Mahwah, NJ. Reprinted by permission of Paulist Press, Inc. www.paulistpress.com.

Page 64: Pope Benedict XVI, General Audience, October 25, 2006. Used with permission of the Libreria Editrice Vaticana. www.vatican.va.

Page 75: Blessed John Paul II, *Rosarium Virginis Mariae (The Rosary of the Virgin Mary)*, 16, Apostolic Letter, October 16, 2002. Used with permission of the Libreria Editrice Vaticana. www.vatican.va.

Page 90: Gallican Formularies, *Hymns to Christ*. © 1982, St. Paul Publications, Slough, SL, UK.

Page 96: Blessed John Paul II, *The Way to Christ: Spiritual Exercises*, Leslie Wearne, Tr. © 1994, HarperOne Publishers, San Francisco, CA.

Page 101: Blessed John Paul II, *Dives in Misericordia (Rich in Mercy:* On the Mercy of God*)*, 13, Encyclical Letter, November 30. © 1980, Pauline Books & Media, Boston, MA. www.pauline.org.

Page 101: Pope Benedict XVI, General Audience, November 8, 2006; General Audience, October 25, 2006. Used with permission of the Libreria Editrice Vaticana. www.vatican.va.

Page 106: Father John Tauler, O.P., *The Following of Christ*, BiblioLife, www.bibliolife.com.

Page 119: Blessed John Paul II, *Ecclesia de Eucharistia (Church of the Eucharist:* On the Eucharist in its Relationship to the Church*)*, 60, Encyclical Letter, April 17, 2003. Used with permission of the Libreria Editrice Vaticana. www.vatican.va.

Page 127: Blessed John Henry Newman, *John Henry Newman, Prayers * Poems * Meditations*. 1989, SPCK, London, UK.

Page 129: Reinhold Niebuhr, *Manual of Prayers*. © 1996, The American College of the Roman Catholic Church in the United States. All rights reserved. Used with permission.

Page 130: Blessed John Paul II, *Redemptoris Missio (The Mission of Christ the Redeemer:* On the Permanent Validity of the Church's Missionary Mandate*)*, 90, 11, Encyclical Letter, December, 7 1990. Used with permission of the Libreria Editrice Vaticana. www.vatican.va.

Page 132: Saint Isaac Jogues, *The Life of Father Isaac Jogues, S.J.*, by Felix Martin, S.J. 1885, Benziger Brothers, New York, NY.

Page 139: Pope Benedict XVI, Address to the Sick at the End of the Mass, February 11, 2006, On the Occasion of the 14th World Day of the Sick. Used with permission of the Libreria Editrice Vaticana. www.vatican.va.

Page 147: Blessed John Paul II, Homily, October 6, 1993, Chapel of Saint Joseph's Seminary, Yonkers, NY. Used with permission of the Libreria Editrice Vaticana. www.vatican.va.

Page 161: Blessed John Paul II, *Laborem Exercens* (On Human Work), 9, Encyclical Letter, September 14, 1991. Used with permission of the Libreria Editrice Vaticana. www.vatican.va.

Page 163: Blessed John Paul II, *Laborem Exercens* (On Human Work), 27, Encyclical Letter, September 14, 1991. Used with permission of the Libreria Editrice Vaticana. www.vatican.va.

Page 166: Blessed John Paul II, *Salvifici Doloris* (On the Christian Meaning of Human Suffering), 26, 27, 30, Apostolic Letter, February 11, 1984. Used with permission of the Libreria Editrice Vaticana. www.vatican.va.

Page 170: Venerable Thomas à Kempis, *The Imitation of Christ*, Aloysius Croft and Harold Bolton, Trs. 2003, Dover Publications, Inc., Mineola, NY.

Page 171: Saint Maximus the Confessor, *Hymns to Christ*. © 1982, St. Paul Publications, Slough, SL, UK.

MAGNIFICAT®